MOVIE STAR HOMES

The Famous to the Forgotten

BH

SUNSET ◄ **BLVD** ►
9600

Judy Artunian and Mike Oldham

S A N T A
M O N I C A
P R E S S

Published by:
Santa Monica Press LLC
P.O. Box 1076
Santa Monica, CA 90406-1076
1-800-784-9553
www.santamonicapress.com
books@santamonicapress.com

Printed in the United States

Santa Monica Press books are available at special quantity discounts when purchased in bulk by corporations, organizations, or groups. Please call our Special Sales department at 1-800-784-9553.

ISBN 1-891661-38-8

Library of Congress Cataloging-in-Publication Data

Artunian, Judy, 1952–
        Movie star homes: the famous to the forgotten / Judy Artunian and Mike Oldham.
        p. cm.
        Includes bibliographical references.
        ISBN 1-891661-38-8
        1. Motion picture actors and actresses—Homes and haunts—California—Los Angeles. 2. Motion picture actors and actresses—Homes and haunts—California, Southern. 3. Los Angeles (Calif.)—Buildings, structures, etc. 4. Dwellings—California—Los Angeles. I. Oldham, Mike, 1958– II. Title.
        PN1993.5.U65A78 2004
        791.4302'8'092279494—dc22

                                                                    2004005596

Book and cover design by Lynda "Cool Dog" Jakovich

TABLE OF CONTENTS

DEDICATION

To Sam Gabrelian

He wasn't a movie star, but it was while looking for Sam's 1916 Los Angeles home address that we stumbled upon one for Lillian Gish. Without that unexpected discovery, this book would not have existed.

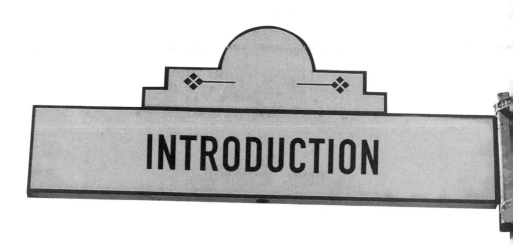

INTRODUCTION

When the term "movie star home" comes up in conversation, most people imagine a grand palace like Brad Pitt's Beverly Hills mansion. But the apartment buildings on the outskirts of Hollywood where the likes of Clark Gable lived in their pre-star days are movie star homes too—albeit of a more humble variety. *Movie Star Homes: The Famous to the Forgotten* gives you a snapshot of the Southern California homes where Hollywood's favorites live and have lived, dating back to the silent era. Our goal was to cover the full spectrum of homes—from the Beverly Hills mansions that are as glamorous as their celebrity occupants, to the now-frayed bungalows of old Hollywood.

Los Angeles realtors like to quip that every house in the city has been occupied by three different movie stars at one time or another. That is only a slight exaggeration. For whatever reason, actors tend to change households only somewhat more often than they change spouses. Since we couldn't include every home of every actor who ever set foot on a Hollywood set, we established three ground rules for determining which homes made the cut.

Our first ground rule was that the home had to be in Southern California. Perhaps someday our budgets will allow us to spend a month in Tahiti looking for Marlon Brando's grass-roofed hut (yes, he does have one).

All of the homes in this book were photographed in 2003 and 2004 by the authors, which leads to our second ground rule: In order to be included in the book, the house that stands today at an actor's address had to be the same structure that the actor lived in, even if it had been remodeled or otherwise spruced up over the years.

This rule eliminated homes like Pickfair, the Beverly Hills estate where Mary Pickford and Douglas Fairbanks, Hollywood's reigning queen and king of the 1920s, held court. You can still drive up to the wrought-iron gates that proclaim "Pickfair" at 1143 Summit Drive, but the mansion you see behind those gates isn't *the* Pickfair where Mary Pickford lived for nearly five decades. The original house was all but leveled in 1991 and rebuilt from the ground up.

Our third ground rule was that the book had to represent the huge variety of homes that have been inhabited by film stars over the years. That is why this book isn't devoted solely to the glitzy estates. Nor, for that matter, is it weighted toward the obscure homes that often hold the most compelling stories. If the selection of homes and actors on these pages seems unpredictable or quirky, it's because the star and/or the home had to resonate with us on some level. Sometimes we were struck by the fragile and forlorn quality of a certain structure (like the downtown Los Angeles building where Rudolph Valentino lived in 1919), and wanted to document its existence before a wrecking ball erases it from the landscape. But just as often our decision about who and what to include after the first three rules were satisfied came down to a sixth sense that defies explanation. We're grateful to our publisher, Jeffrey Goldman, for allowing us to follow our instincts. That is what makes this ultimately a highly personal book, and one that we hope will contain many happy discoveries for you, the reader.

Unearthing these addresses and confirming their accuracy sometimes required painstaking gumshoe detective work. On this note, we wish to salute Steve McQueen, whose Solar Drive address took hours of tedious research to find and authenticate. Just as his *Great Escape* character, Captain Virgil Hilts, almost eluded his captors, McQueen almost escaped *Movie Star Homes.* (But Steve, we gotcha!)

From the day three years ago when we first realized that there is a treasure trove of movie star homes to be discovered and rediscovered, we've gotten a kick out of the residential discoveries that seemed to be waiting for us around every corner.

We hope that you'll find a few surprises of your own as you take your tour of *Movie Star Homes: The Famous to the Forgotten.*

A few "housekeeping" notes:

The houses in this book are organized alphabetically by the actors' last names. Each entry includes a brief profile of the actor, the street address of the featured home (in some cases you'll find two homes for one actor), a photo of the home as it looks today, and facts or anecdotes about the home or the actor's home life.

Many of the homes pictured in this book are in the city of Los Angeles. When a residence is located in a specific region of the city, such as Silver Lake or Bel Air, we list it as being in that region, rather than in Los Angeles. The boundaries of the various regions vary, depending on the map you consult. In the cases where a home appears to be on the border between two regions, we used our best judgment in deciding where to place it. The actors are listed by region in the Appendix, beginning on page 291. In the Appendix, we also suggest special "tours" you can take to find the homes of some of your favorite stars. To get detailed directions to specific homes, we suggest that you consult MapQuest (www.mapquest.com) or *Thomas Guide: Los Angeles & Orange Counties,* a map book that is available at most bookstores.

Regarding when the actors lived in the homes featured in this book: We provide only the years for which we could confirm the actors' occupancy. Some may have lived at a particular address for a longer period of time.

One last, but important, note: Please respect the privacy of the occupants of the homes listed in this book.

Judy Artunian and Mike Oldham
May 2004

Bud Abbott (1895–1974)
12808 Halkirk Street, Studio City

Bud Abbott, the straight man in the Abbott & Costello comedy team, first worked with Lou Costello when he took the place of Costello's ailing partner. In 1940, they made a brief appearance in *One Night in the Tropics*. It was their first movie and also the first time they performed their famous "Who's on First" routine in a film.

This Studio City home, built by Abbott in 1939, includes a separate guest-house. The estate was on the market in 2003 for $1.15 million. Abbott resided in at least four different San Fernando Valley homes from the late 1930s until his death in 1974. Like his partner, Lou Costello, Abbott was forced to sell one of his homes during the 1950s in order to pay back taxes to the Internal Revenue Service.

June Allyson (1917–)
3100 Mandeville Canyon Road, Brentwood

June Allyson starred in a string of World War II-era films, such as *Two Girls and a Sailor* (1944), which showcased her flair for playing the upbeat, virtuous

girl next door. Allyson is also remembered for *The Glenn Miller Story* (1954), in which she portrayed the wife of the doomed title character, played by James Stewart.

Allyson's husband, actor Dick Powell, picked out this Mandeville Canyon estate in the early 1950s. In her memoir, Allyson recalled that Powell drove her to the remote property and asked if it was too isolated for her. "Heavens no," she said. "It's a nice community. How many people live here?" Powell's response: "Just us, Junie. It's our 68 acres."

Don Ameche (1908–1993)
4684 White Oak Avenue, Encino

Don Ameche first appeared on screen in *The Sins of Man* (1936), and wrapped up his career 58 years later in *Corrina, Corrina* (1994), which was released after his death. Along the way, Ameche played everything from amiable ladies' men to a singing musketeer. At the age of 80 he earned an Academy Award for Best Supporting Actor for his work in *Cocoon* (1988). It was

his first Oscar.

Ameche owned the Spanish-style house at the end of this driveway during the 1930s and 1940s. W.C. Fields rented the house in the 1930s. A second story was added in 2003.

Eddie "Rochester" Anderson (1905–1977)
1932 Rochester Circle, Los Angeles

"Oh Rochester!" That was a familiar refrain to Jack Benny fans. The Rochester in question was Benny's right-hand man, played by Eddie Anderson. Anderson matched wits with Benny in several movies and on Benny's radio and TV shows. Anderson also played supporting roles in *You Can't Take It with You* (1938) and *Gone With the Wind* (1939).

Anderson lived in this regal home while he was co-starring in *The Jack Benny* TV series during the 1950s. The city re-named a portion of West 37th Street "Rochester Circle" in Anderson's honor.

Dana Andrews (1909–1992)
451-B North Doheny Drive, Beverly Hills

Dana Andrews was part of the stellar cast of the post-World War II drama *The Best Years of Our Lives* (1946). In the movie, which won the Academy Award for Best Picture, Andrews plays the war veteran who dumps his superficial wife in favor of Theresa Wright. Andrews' many other films include *The Ox-Bow Incident* (1943), *Where the Sidewalk Ends*

(1956) and *Night of the Demon* (1957).

In 1940, the first year of his film career, Andrews lived in unit B in this small apartment building on Doheny Drive. Palm trees and tall shrubbery stand between the building and the street.

Julie Andrews (1935–)
9531 Hidden Valley Road, Los Angeles

Julie Andrews won the Best Actress Oscar for her very first movie, *Mary Poppins* (1964). She continued to win raves for her performances in such movies as *The Sound of Music* (1965), *S.O.B.* (1981) and *Victor/Victoria* (1982), in which she played a man who impersonates a woman.

In the early 1960s, Julie Andrews moved into this brick and wood house that is tucked away in the appropriately titled Hidden Valley area of Los Angeles. Hidden Valley Road has been home to other stars, including Rex Harrison and Myrna Loy.

Julie Andrews
9531 Hidden Valley Road, Los Angeles

Ann-Margret (1941–)
2707 Benedict Canyon Drive, Los Angeles

Ann-Margret's energetic display of song and dance talent in *Bye Bye Birdie* (1963) made her a star practically overnight. She proceeded to win roles in the

Elvis Presley vehicle, *Viva Las Vegas* (1964), as well as *Carnal Knowledge* (1971), *Grumpy Old Men* (1993) and *Any Given Sunday* (1999).

Ann-Margret and her husband, actor Roger Smith, bought this estate in the late 1960s. The Cape Cod-style house sits on 10 acres. The estate originally belonged to Hedy Lamarr in the 1940s, and it was Lamarr who named the property "Hedgerow." Humphrey Bogart and Lauren Bacall also lived here at one point.

Roscoe "Fatty" Arbuckle (1887–1933)
649 West Adams Boulevard, Los Angeles

Fatty Arbuckle is one of film comedy's forgotten pioneers. Arbuckle made his first movie in 1909 and soon became known for his knock-about style of slapstick. His career was cut short by a rape charge. Although he was acquitted in two trials, moviegoers and the studios turned against him. Toward the end of his life, Arbuckle worked behind the scenes under assumed names, such as "Will B. Good."

Arbuckle's West Adams estate passed through several celebrity hands. Arbuckle bought the property from actress Theda Bara in 1918. In 1922, he sold the estate to director Raoul Walsh and his wife, actress Miriam Cooper, who later sold it to actress Norma Talmadge and her husband, producer Joe Schenck.

Roscoe "Fatty" Arbuckle
649 West Adams Boulevard, Los Angeles

Eve Arden (1908–1990)
7044 Los Tilos Road, Hollywood Hills

Eve Arden was a master at playing no-nonsense women with a pungent wit. She was cast in supporting roles in such movies as *Stage Door* (1937), *Cover Girl* (1944) and *Mildred Pierce* (1945). Arden also starred in the popular *Our Miss Brooks* TV series from 1952–1956.

In the 1940s, while Arden's career was in full swing, she and her first husband, Ned Bergen, lived in this house located at the top of a winding Hollywood Hills road.

Fred Astaire (1899–1987)
1155 San Ysidro Drive, Beverly Hills

Film historians often say that Fred Astaire single-handedly breathed new life into the movie musical when he came to Hollywood in the early 1930s. Through the creative dance numbers he choreographed with Hermes Pan, Astaire advanced the art of expressing emotion on screen through dance. Ginger Rogers was his partner for most of his best-loved movies, including *Top Hat* (1935), *Swing Time* (1936) and *Shall We Dance* (1937).

Astaire built this house in 1960 and lived here until his death, 27 years later. Unlike the lavish art deco interiors of his film characters' penthouse apartments, Astaire's homes were more traditional. His dining room, for example, featured period English furniture.

Eve Arden
7044 Los Tilos Road, Hollywood Hills

Mary Astor (1906–1987)
2056 North Sycamore Avenue, Hollywood Hills

Mary Astor may be best remembered as the conniving Brigid who was tripped up by Humphrey Bogart in *The Maltese Falcon* (1941). Astor's long film career included

an Academy Award for her role in *The Great Lie* (1941). Earlier in her career she starred opposite John Barrymore in *Beau Brummel* (1924) and *Don Juan* (1925), and opposite Clark Gable in *Red Dust* (1932).

Astor lived here in the 1950s. The house is just up the block from the Yamashiro Gardens. As a teenager, Astor lived with her parents in a Hollywood house which had previously been rented by Charlie Chaplin (6147 Temple Hill Drive—see Charlie Chaplin).

Gene Autry (1907–1998)
3171 Brookdale Road, Studio City

Gene Autry, known as "The Singing Cowboy," parlayed his musical and dramatic talents into successful careers in radio, movies, TV and the record industry. Autry made 94 movies between 1934 and 1959. He wrote many of the songs he performed on screen, including "Back in the Saddle Again," from the movie *Back in the Saddle* (1941). Autry later cofounded the Anaheim Angels baseball team.

In 1949, Autry and his wife, Ina, built this Studio City house. Today, the front gate still sports the lassoed "A"—the logo for Autry's Flying A Productions. The house is on a four-acre lot Autry purchased before World War II.

Lauren Bacall (1924–)
10430 Bellagio Road, Bel Air

Lauren Bacall's cool demeanor and exotic looks were a perfect fit for her roles opposite future husband Humphrey Bogart in such films as *To Have and Have Not* (1944) and *The Big Sleep* (1946). In later years, Bacall appeared in *The Shootist* (1976), opposite John Wayne, and *The Mirror Has Two Faces* (1996), in which she played Barbara Streisand's mother.

Bacall moved to this house after Bogart died. She was enamored of California homes. In her second memoir, Bacall wrote, "The amazing thing to me about California, after having been born and brought up in New York, totally cement-, elevator-, bus-, and subway-oriented, was that I could open my front or back door and walk directly onto a lawn."

Lucille Ball (1911–1989)
1344 North Ogden Drive, West Hollywood
1000 North Roxbury Drive, Beverly Hills

Lucille Ball's comedic talents are evident in her earliest films. She squared off against the Marx Brothers in *Room Service* (1938), and co-starred with Bob Hope in *Sorrowful Jones* (1949) and *Fancy Pants* (1950). In 1951, Ball left movies for TV when she and husband, Desi Arnaz, launched the *I Love Lucy* TV series (1951–1957).

1344 North Ogden Drive: In 1934, Ball rented this house in West Hollywood. She brought her family out from the Midwest to live with her in those early days of her career.

1000 North Roxbury Drive: Ball and Arnaz bought this Beverly Hills mansion next door to Jack Benny in 1954. They had been living on a ranch in Chatsworth since the mid-1940s, but wanted to be closer to the studio where their TV show was being shot. They sold the ranch to actress Jane Withers.

Lucille Ball
1000 North Roxbury Drive, Beverly Hills

Anne Bancroft (1931–)
8365 Sunset View Drive, Hollywood Hills

After Anne Bancroft's Tony-winning performance as Helen Keller's teacher in the Broadway production of *The Miracle Worker,* director Arthur Penn asked her to play the same role in the 1962 movie version of the hit play. Bancroft won the Academy Award for Best Supporting Actress for that performance. Six years later she made a splash as the middle-aged Mrs. Robinson who seduces Dustin Hoffman in *The Graduate* (1967).

Bancroft and her husband, filmmaker Mel Brooks, have had a part-time home on this property since the 1960s. Their house isn't visible from the street. Passersby can see only the maid's quarters in front of the main house.

Theda Bara (1885–1955)
632 North Alpine Drive, Beverly Hills

Theda Bara is often called the movies' first sex symbol. She created an exotic image by inventing a mysterious Egyptian heritage, wearing heavy eye makeup and starring in costume dramas like *Camille* (1917) and *Cleopatra* (1917). She was a screen sensation until 1920, when audiences apparently tired of her exotic vamp image.

Bara moved to this house—with its Tudor-style touches—after marrying director Charles Brabin in 1921. She previously lived in the West Adams district of Los Angeles (649 West Adams Boulevard— see Fatty Arbuckle).

Theda Bara
632 North Alpine Drive, Beverly Hills

Lex Barker (1919–1973)
120 South Mapleton Drive, Holmby Hills

Lex Barker followed Johnny Weissmuller as Tarzan. He starred in five Tarzan films, starting with *Tarzan's Magic Fountain* (1949). A year earlier, Barker played

Cary Grant's contractor in *Mr. Blandings Builds His Dream House* (1948). In later years, he worked mostly in Europe, where one of his coups was a part in Fellini's classic, *La Dolce Vita* (1961).

Barker lived in this house in the 1950s.

Drew Barrymore (1975–)
360 North Martel Avenue, Los Angeles

Drew Barrymore first won the hearts of movie audiences when she played six-year-old Gertie in *E. T. The Extra-Terrestrial* (1982). As an adult, Barrymore has starred in *Never Been Kissed* (1999), *Charlie's Angels* (2000) and its sequel, *Charlie's Angels Full Throttle* (2003). She has also served as executive producer for several of her movies. Barrymore's grandfather was famed thespian John Barrymore, and her grandmother was actress Dolores Costello.

Barrymore's former house on Martel Avenue is locked away behind a leafy wall. In 2001, a Beverly Hills-area house she shared with then-fiancé, Tom Green, burned to the ground. Barrymore credited their dog, Flossie, for waking them up in time to escape unharmed.

John Barrymore (1882–1942)
Ambassador Hotel
3400 Wilshire Boulevard, Los Angeles

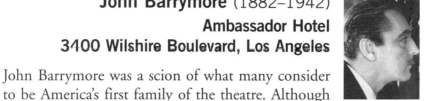

John Barrymore was a scion of what many consider to be America's first family of the theatre. Although he was known as the "The Great Profile," Barrymore was fond of movie roles that allowed him to disappear into grotesque or disheveled characters. Among Barrymore's best-loved films are *Dr. Jekyll and Mr. Hyde* (1920) and *The Twentieth Century* (1934).

During much of the 1920s, Barrymore made his home at the Ambassador Hotels in Los Angeles and New York City. (The Los Angeles Ambassador, shown here as it looked in 2003, now belongs to the Los Angeles Unified School District.) In 1927, he purchased a house near Beverly Hills on three acres (the house has since been torn down). He then bought four adjacent acres and named his estate "Bella Vista." Barrymore brought his pet monkey, Clementine, and his manager, Henry Hotchner, with him while he was house hunting. He reportedly told Hotchner, "All the swells live in Beverly Hills. Why should Clementine reside in a lower social environment?"

Lionel Barrymore (1878–1954)
800 North Roxbury Drive, Beverly Hills

Lionel Barrymore divided his time between the Broadway stage and movies for a decade before settling on what would become a distinguished movie career. Barrymore frequently played unlikable characters, such as the unscrupulous physician in *Body and Soul* (1927), the grouchy Dr. Gillespie in the *Dr. Kildare* movies (1938–1942) and the greedy Mr. Potter in *It's a Wonderful Life* (1946). Among his more sympathetic roles were the terminally ill businessman in *Grand Hotel* (1932), and the kindly father in *You Can't Take It with You* (1938). Barrymore was the older brother of actors John and Ethyl Barrymore.

Barrymore lived here from the late 1920s until 1936. In his day, the address was 802 North Roxbury. He was three miles from his brother, John, who was known for his carousing. Lionel wrote in his memoir, "My wife and I lived quietly on Roxbury Drive, Beverly Hills. Jack lived unquietly on Tower Rd."

Richard Barthelmess (1895–1963)
Los Angeles Athletic Club
431 West Seventh Street, Los Angeles

Handsome Richard Barthelmess became a major box-office favorite after wooing Lillian Gish in *Broken*

Blossoms (1919) and *Way Down East* (1920). Among the most admired of Barthelmess' talking picture performances was *Only Angels Have Wings* (1939) with Rita Hayworth.

In 1919, Barthelmess lived at the Los Angeles Athletic Club in downtown Los Angeles. The Athletic Club was also a popular hangout for stars like Rudolph Valentino, Douglas Fairbanks, Jr., and Johnny Weissmuller.

Lionel Barrymore
800 North Roxbury Drive, Beverly Hills

Kim Basinger (1953–)
4833 Don Juan Place, Woodland Hills

A former Georgia Junior Miss turned supermodel, Kim Basinger's first major movie role was the quirky title character in *Nadine* (1987). She then landed the part of Vickie Vale in *Batman* (1989). Eight years later Basinger won

the Best Supporting Actress Oscar for her portrayal of the seductive Lynn Bracken in *L.A. Confidential* (1997).

This house, owned by Basinger since the 1980s, is located on a Woodland Hills cul-de-sac. A black wrought-iron fence surrounds the house.

Kathy Bates (1948–)
2829 Westshire Drive, Hollywood Hills

Character actress Kathy Bates earned an Academy Award for Best Actress for portraying the psychotic fan of an author played by James Caan in *Misery* (1990). Bates also co-starred in *Dolores Claiborne* (1995), *Primary Colors* (1998) and *About Schmidt* (2002).

Bates lived in this English Country-style house in the Hollywood Hills in the 1990s. In early 2000 she sold it to actor Jon Cryer.

Anne Baxter (1923–1985)
8650 Pine Tree Place, Hollywood Hills

Anne Baxter's most acclaimed role was that of the scheming Eve, opposite Bette Davis, in *All About Eve* (1950). Four years earlier, Baxter won an Academy Award for Best Supporting Actress for *The Razor's Edge* (1946).

In 1946, Baxter's grandfather, pioneering architect Frank Lloyd Wright, designed and supervised the renovation of this house as a wedding gift to Baxter and her husband, actor John Hodiak.

Warner Baxter (1889–1951)
911 North Roxbury Drive, Beverly Hills

After Warner Baxter won the Academy Award for Best Actor for his portrayal of the bandit Cisco Kid in *In Old Arizona* (1929), he played the same role in four more movies. He also co-starred with Janet Gaynor in *Daddy Long Legs* (1931), and with Freddie Bartholomew in *Kidnapped* (1938). But Baxter's biggest claim to fame may be a single line he delivered in the film version of the musical *42nd Street* (1933). When the understudy dancer, played by Ruby Keeler, is about to make her grand stage entrance, Baxter, playing the no-nonsense director, tells her, "Sawyer, you're going out there a youngster, but you've got to come back a star!"

By the 1940s, Baxter had downsized to this mansion in Beverly Hills. A decade earlier, when his career was at its zenith, he lived in a Tudor-style mansion that sat on four acres in Bel Air.

Warren Beatty (1937–)
Regent Beverly Wilshire Hotel
9500 Wilshire Boulevard, Beverly Hills
12431 Mulholland Drive, Los Angeles

Warren Beatty started out as a conventional leading man, but developed into an accomplished filmmaker. He earned both producer and star credits for what would become his signature role—bank robber Clyde Barrow in *Bonnie and Clyde* (1967). Beatty continued tackling a diverse range of characters and often served as writer, director and/or producer for such films as *McCabe and Mrs. Miller* (1971), *Shampoo* (1975), *Heaven Can Wait* (1978), *Reds* (1981) and *Bugsy* (1991). Beatty won the Academy Award for Best Director for *Reds*.

Regent Beverly Wilshire: Beatty lived for years at the Regent Beverly Wilshire. In the mid-1970s, after moving into his first house, Beatty commented to a writer, "I still like living in the hotel. It's easier. Everyone likes to make a big deal out of my buying a house. They think it shows some kind of maturity. I see [needing roots] as immaturity…I'm already bored with the house."

12431 Mulholland Drive: Beatty has lived here since the early 1990s. From the street you can see a driveway that is sheltered by over-hanging trees. The estate is near the busy intersection of Mulholland Drive and Coldwater Canyon Drive.

Ralph Bellamy (1904–1991)
609 North Canon Drive, Beverly Hills

Ralph Bellamy became pegged as the actor to cast when a script called for a guy who doesn't get the girl. Bellamy turned in memorable performances in such

movies as *The Magnificent Lie* (1931), *The Awful Truth* (1937) and *His Girl Friday* (1940). In his later years, Bellamy appeared in *Trading Places* (1983) and *Pretty Woman* (1990).

Bellamy lived in this Canon Drive house during the 1940s. As a young man, he and fellow actor Charles Farrell liked to get away to Palm Springs between pictures. In 1932, they bought property in the desert city and built a couple of tennis courts. They decided to form a club as a way to defray some of their costs. To their surprise, it became a favorite gathering spot for Hollywood actors and grew into a posh resort called the Racquet Club of Palm Springs.

Annette Bening (1958–)
12431 Mulholland Drive, Los Angeles

Annette Bening won the Academy Award for Best Actress for her portrayal of the chilly, super-stressed Carol in *American Beauty* (1999). Her first brush with an Oscar came nine years earlier when she was nominated for her supporting role in *The Grifters* (1990). Bening met future husband, Warren Beatty, when she played Bugsy Segal's sultry girlfriend in *Bugsy* (1991).

After the 1994 Northridge earthquake destroyed an earlier home, Bening and her husband, Warren Beatty, bought this estate, which is dominated by a Spanish-Mediterranean mansion.

Joan Bennett (1910–1990)
515 South Mapleton Drive, Holmby Hills

Joan Bennett didn't approach star status until 1938, when she changed her hair color from blond to brunette at the urging of producer Walter Wanger (who she later married). Sporting her newly colored locks, Bennett landed major roles in *The Man with the Iron Mask* (1939), *Father of the Bride* (1950) and other favorites.

Bennett hired noted architect Wallace Neff to design this French Provincial-style house in 1937. In 1943, the house nearly burned to the ground. It took more than a year to rebuild it to match the original architecture.

Jack Benny (1894–1974)
1002 North Roxbury Drive, Beverly Hills

Comedian Jack Benny was a fixture in American living rooms thanks to his popular radio show, when Paramount nabbed him for the movies. In addition to starring with his radio cast in several movies, Benny performed separately in such hits as *Charley's Aunt* (1941), *To Be or Not To Be* (1942) and *Without Reservations* (1946).

Benny built this Georgian Colonial-style home in 1938, and lived here for nearly 30 years. It took him a while to get used to the home's secu-

rity system. His daughter recalled in her memoir that he was prone to accidentally activating the alarm that went directly to the Beverly Hills Police Station, when he had actually intended to press the buttons that called his butler or maid.

Candice Bergen (1946–)
9897 Beverly Grove Drive, Los Angeles

Candice Bergen earned strong reviews for *Carnal Knowledge* (1971) and her Academy Award-nominated performance as Burt Reynolds ex-wife in *Starting Over* (1979). She divided her time between photojournalism and acting for many years. In 1988, Bergen began her 10-year reign as the title character in the *Murphy Brown* TV series.

As a child, Bergen, the daughter of the popular ventriloquist Edgar Bergen, used to play on the grounds of the old John Barrymore estate. In 1973, she bought a house located beyond this driveway. The house had served as Barrymore's aviary and was one of three houses on the property. Bergen wrote in her memoir: "Filled with fantasy and whimsy, the Aviary was the most impractical of the three, and this, of course was the one I wanted. Katharine Hepburn had lived in the Aviary, and Marlon Brando; the little house was heavy with Hollywood history."

Edgar Bergen (1903–1978)
9876 Beverly Grove Drive, Los Angeles

Ventriloquist Edgar Bergen and his alter ego, the wisecracking wooden "dummy" Charlie McCarthy, starred in several shorts before landing roles in features such as W.C. Fields' *You Can't Cheat an Honest Man* (1941). Bergen eventually added the dummy Mortimer Snerd to his ensemble.

The Bergen family called this hacienda-style house "Bella Vista." They lived here from the 1940s on. Walls surrounded the hilltop house. His daughter, actress Candice Bergen, wrote in her memoir that "'Bella Vista' was not readily accessible to the timid or fainthearted."

Ingrid **Bergman** (1915–1982)
260 South Camden Drive, Beverly Hills

After breaking into films in her native Sweden, Ingrid Bergman came to Hollywood. She appeared in such hits as *Casablanca* (1942) and *For Whom the Bell Tolls* (1943), then won an Oscar for Best Actress for *Gaslight* (1944). She also earned Academy Awards for *Anastasia* (1956) and *Murder on the Orient Express* (1974).

In 1939, when producer David O. Selznick brought Bergman from Sweden to the United States to be one of his new leading ladies, he leased this Spanish-style villa for her. Selznick also hired a woman to stay with her and serve as her cook, driver and personal assistant. Bergman was enchanted by the house's red-tile roof, arched porticos and the lemon, olive and eucalyptus trees on the property.

Joan **Blondell** (1906–1979)
711 North Maple Drive, Beverly Hills

Joan Blondell perfected the role of the fast-talking "dame" who populated many depression-era movies. Blondell played opposite James Cagney in *The Public Enemy* (1931) and *Footlight Parade* (1933). She also appeared in *Three on a Match* (1932) with Bette Davis, and *Gold Diggers of 1937* (1936) with her first husband, Dick Powell.

Blondell and Powell lived here in 1936. "My home has always been foremost in my life," she once said. "They made jokes about it at Warner Brothers because the moment they said 'Cut!' I was out of that studio and into my car and zip through the gate!"

Ingrid Bergman
260 South Camden Drive, Beverly Hills

Eric Blore (1887–1959)
333 24th Street, Santa Monica

Eric Blore played humorously imperious butlers and managers in many Fred Astaire-Ginger Rogers musicals, including *Top Hat* (1935) and *Swing Time* (1936). After arriving in Hollywood from London in the mid-1920s, Blore landed his first American movie role, playing Lord Digby in *The Great Gatsby* (1926).

The Pacific coast is within four miles of this gray-and-white house where Blore lived during the 1930s.

Monte Blue (1887–1963)
716 North Camden Drive, Beverly Hills

Monte Blue made his screen debut as a stuntman in D.W. Griffith films. After co-starring with Dorothy and Lillian Gish in *Orphans of the Storm* (1921), Blue became one of the silent era's most popular romantic leading men. He lost most of his fortune in the 1929 stock market crash. At about the same time, his movie opportunities dwindled to the point to where he was again working as a stuntman.

Today, true to its early owner's name, Blue's Camden Drive house is painted a very light blue. The house is in the heart of one of the earliest housing developments in Beverly Hills. Blue lived here in the 1920s.

Monte Blue
716 North Camden Drive, Beverly Hills

Humphrey Bogart (1899–1957)
232 South Mapleton Drive, Holmby Hills

When Humphrey Bogart brought the snarling thug, Duke Mantee, from the Broadway stage to the film version of *The Petrified Forest* (1936), moviegoers got their first look at what would become one of Humphrey Bogart's mainstay characters. Since then, Bogart films such as *The Maltese*

Falcon (1941), *Casablanca* (1942), *The Treasure of the Sierra Madre* (1948) and *The African Queen* (1951) have taken on identities of their own. Bogart earned the Best Actor Oscar for *The African Queen.*

In the 1950s, Bogart and his wife, actress Lauren Bacall, lived in this Holmby Hills house. The Bogarts installed a swimming pool, and the handprints of their two children may still be visible in the concrete surrounding the pool.

Ray Bolger (1904–1987)
618 North Beverly Drive, Beverly Hills

Ray Bolger's loose-limbed dancing style made him a natural for the good-natured, feather-light Scarecrow in *The Wizard of Oz* (1939). Bolger refined his song and dance

skills in vaudeville and on Broadway. In addition to *The Wizard of Oz*, Bolger appeared in *The Great Ziegfeld* (1936), and re-teamed with Judy Garland in *The Harvey Girls* (1946).

Bolger lived in this white house with black trim during the 1950s. It was just a fireball's throw from the Canon Drive home of Margaret Hamilton, which no longer stands. Hamilton played the Wicked Witch of the West, who set fire to Bolger's Scarecrow character in *The Wizard of Oz.*

Shirley Booth (1898–1992)
2276 Bowmont Drive, Los Angeles

Shirley Booth was a Tony Award-winning stage actress for 25 years before Hollywood came calling. Booth won the Best Actress Oscar for her first film role, the

beleaguered Lola in *Come Back, Little Sheba* (1952). It was a part she had made famous on Broadway. She later starred in TV's *Hazel* (1960–66).

In the 1960s, Booth resided off of Coldwater Canyon Boulevard in this white house that sits today behind a white wall and green fence. The house is situated at a fork that splits Bowmont Drive and Hazen Drive.

Olive Borden (1907–1947)
627 North Hillcrest Road, Beverly Hills

For about two years during the roaring twenties, Olive Borden was one of Hollywood's hottest young actresses. Among her most popular films were *Fig Leaves* (1926), an early directing effort by Howard Hawks, and *The Joy Girl* (1927). Borden's fortunes changed when she refused to take

the salary offered by her studio, Fox. She went on to win movie roles elsewhere, but her career was short-lived. After serving in the WACS during World War II, Borden was reduced to jobs like scrubbing floors.

In the mid-1920s, Borden lived in style in this Beverly Hills home. Twenty years later, she ended her days living in a downtown Los Angeles shelter for homeless women.

Ernest Borgnine (1917–)
13531 Vose Street, Van Nuys

Although he was often cast as an unsympathetic character, Ernest Borgnine's poignant performance as a lonely bachelor in *Marty* (1955) earned him the Academy Award for Best Actor. Borgnine was also featured in *The Dirty Dozen*

(1967), *The Poseidon Adventure* (1972) and on the TV series, *McHale's Navy* (1962–1966).

Borgnine lived in this unassuming San Fernando Valley house through much of the 1950s while his career was in full swing.

Clara Bow (1905–1965)
512 North Bedford Drive, Beverly Hills

Auburn-haired Clara Bow, a.k.a. the "It Girl," personified the free-spirited flapper of the roaring twenties. She starred in films like *The Plastic Age* (1925) and the appropriately titled *It* (1927). In the mid-1930s, after marrying Western star Rex Bell (who later became Nevada's Lieutenant Governor), Bow left Hollywood for a Nevada ranch.

Bow bought this house in 1926. A visiting journalist described the house as "… an ordinary stucco bungalow, but inside it is exactly like Clara. The beautiful and the bizarre, the exquisite and the commonplace, mingled in hopeless confusion."

Clara Bow
512 North Bedford Drive, Beverly Hills

William Boyd (1895–1972)
2010 Vine Street, Hollywood Hills

He starred as a matinee idol in the 1920s, but William Boyd made his mark by playing the clean-cut cowboy Hopalong Cassidy between 1935 and 1948. He made 66 Hopalong Cassidy movies, and later starred as the same character on radio and TV. Boyd bought the rights to all of his films, and

earned royalties for many years from Hopalong Cassidy comic books and other products.

Boyd's Vine Street house, where he lived in the 1930s, is within a mile of the famed intersection of Hollywood and Vine. Coincidentally, Boyd's star on the Hollywood Walk of Fame is on Vine Street, about halfway between his house and the famous intersection.

Marlon Brando (1924–)
8142 Laurel View Drive, Hollywood Hills

Marlon Brando's celebrated film career took off with his second movie, *A Streetcar Named Desire* (1951), in which he played the explosive Stanley Kowolski. He continued to play characters whose rebellious nature mirrored aspects of his real-life personality. Among Brando's other notable films: *On the Waterfront* (1954), *The Godfather* (1972) and *Apocalypse Now* (1979). He received Best Actor Oscars for *On the Waterfront* and *The Godfather*.

This Spanish-style Hollywood Hills house is distinctive for its scalloped cornice along the top. Brando lived here while he made two major hits, *Teahouse of the August Moon* (1957) and *Sayonara* (1958).

Marlon Brando
8142 Laurel View Drive, Hollywood Hills

Jeff Bridges (1949–)
436 Adelaide Drive, Santa Monica

Jeff Bridges won praise for his portrayals of a lounge singer (with brother Beau Bridges) in *The Fabulous Baker Boys* (1989), a professor who is menaced by his neighbors in *Arlington Road* (1999), and a racehorse owner in *Seabiscuit* (2003). Bridges, the son of actor Lloyd Bridges, was nominated for Best Supporting Actor for his role in *The Last Picture Show* (1971).

Bridges and his family occupied this Santa Monica home for about 13 years before switching to a more remote locale in the mid-1990s. The Santa Monica house had a black-bottom pool and views of the ocean and canyons.

Charles Bronson (1920–2003)
121 Udine Way, Bel Air

After nearly a decade of supporting roles that received minimal attention, Charles Bronson sent his career into high gear with compelling performances in *The*

Magnificent Seven (1960), *The Great Escape* (1963) and *The Dirty Dozen* (1967). He proceeded to star in hard-edged action movies, including *Death Wish* (1974), which sparked controversy for its then-unprecedented violence.

Before they married in 1968, Bronson and his wife, actress Jill Ireland, bought this "fixer-upper" near UCLA. In her memoir, Ireland recalled her first impression of the Udine Way house—"It was nothing less than a mansion; albeit shabby and run down—otherwise Charlie could never have afforded it."

Jeff Bridges
436 Adelaide Drive, Santa Monica

Louise Brooks (1906–1985)
Mi Casa Apartments
1400–1414 Havenhurst Drive, West Hollywood

With her dramatic dark eyes and straight, bobbed hair, Louise Brooks looked like an exotic flapper. In the 1920s, Brooks played flappers, but she also took chances in films

like *Beggars of Life* (1928), in which she played a woman on the lam who tries to pass as a boy. Her most sensational roles were in two racy German movies—*Pandora's Box* (1929) and *Diary of a Lost Girl* (1929).

Brooks lived at the Ronda Apartments in West Hollywood during the 1930s. Now called Mi Casa Apartments, the tile-roofed building features windows of varying shapes and sizes. While Brooks was married to director Eddie Sutherland in the late 1920s, their Laurel Canyon mansion was a hot party spot.

Mel Brooks (1926–)
8365 Sunset View Drive, Hollywood Hills

After years of comedy writing for other entertainers, including TV personality Sid Caesar, Mel Brooks wrote and directed his first feature film, *The Producers* (1968). That was followed by movies like *Blazing Saddles* (1974),

Young Frankenstein (1974) and *High Anxiety* (1978), which parodied classic film genres.

The part-time home of Brooks and his wife, actress Anne Bancroft, since the 1960s, features a pool and a view of the Sunset Strip. Only the maid's quarters are visible from the street.

Joe E. Brown (1892–1973)
707 Walden Drive, Beverly Hills

Joe E. Brown, instantly recognizable by his clown-like face, was featured in comedies throughout the 1930s and 1940s as a loveable buffoon. He starred in *Elmer the Great* (1933), a baseball-themed story that Brown, a huge fan of the sport, would later perform on stage and radio. Brown was also memorable as the rich goofball in *Some Like It Hot* (1959). After proposing to Jack Lemmon and learning that Lemmon isn't a woman, Brown utters the movie's famous last line, "Well, nobody's perfect!"

Brown was a serious collector of sports trophies. He amassed so many trophies, he built a special room in this Beverly Hills home (where he lived from the mid-1930s) to display his collection. Brown called it his "Room of Love."

John Mack Brown (1904–1974)
1119 Calle Vista Drive, Beverly Hills

John Mack Brown played the lead in the *Rough Rider* Western series between 1943 and 1952. During the silent and early sound eras, the former University of Alabama football star was cast in leading-man roles in movies like *Our Dancing Daughters* (1928) starring Joan Crawford, and *A Lady of Chance* (1928) with Norma Shearer.

Brown lived here during the 1940s, when he was a Monogram Studios cowboy star. Today, the 7,000-square-foot house is sequestered behind the green gates that are visible from the street.

Nigel Bruce (1895–1953)
701 North Alpine Drive, Beverly Hills

Nigel Bruce played Dr. Watson in 14 Sherlock Holmes movies, starting with *Hound of the Baskervilles* (1939). Bruce portrayed more devilish characters in *Rebecca* (1940) and *Suspicion* (1941). The British actor also has the distinction of appearing in the first 3-D movie ever released, *Bwana Devil* (1952).

This house, where Bruce lived in the 1930s and 1940s, is situated just south of Sunset. It's about seven miles from the 1930's home of his on-screen partner in crime solving, Basil Rathbone, who played Sherlock Holmes.

Billie Burke (1885–1970)
205 South Woodburn Drive, Brentwood

Billie Burke played chatty, scatterbrained women in comedies such as *Dinner at Eight* (1933) and several *Topper* movies (1937, 1939, 1941). She stepped out of her typecasting when she played Good Witch Glenda in *The Wizard of Oz* (1939), a role she called her favorite.

Burke lived in this Brentwood home for many years until her death in 1970. Prior to that she lived in Beverly Hills with her husband, Broadway producer Florenz Ziegfeld. One of Burke's favorite pastimes was cleaning her house.

Billie Burke
205 South Woodburn Drive, Brentwood

Steve Buscemi (1957–)
1575 Haslam Terrace, Hollywood Hills

Character actor Steve Buscemi specializes in parts that call for strange, vaguely dangerous-looking men. A former New York City firefighter who worked in experimental theatre and performance art, Buscemi played the char-

acter in *Fargo* (1996) who met with an unfortunate fate in a wood chipper.

Buscemi's house is situated on a ledge high above the Sunset Strip. He bought the home in 1993.

Mae Busch (1891–1946)
Hillview Apartments
6531-35 Hollywood Boulevard, Hollywood

Laurel & Hardy devotees know Mae Busch as Oliver Hardy's livid wife in *Son's of the Desert* (1933), one of her

many roles in Laurel & Hardy comedies. During the silent era she was featured in Erich Von Stroheim's *The Devil's Passkey* (1920), and appeared opposite Lon Chaney in *The Unholy Three* (1925).

Busch made her home at the Hillview Apartments in the

1920s. Movie producer Jesse Lasky built the apartment house in 1917. It was home to many actors during the roaring twenties, including Oliver Hardy and Viola Dana.

James Cagney (1899–1986)
1315½ North Hayworth Avenue
West Hollywood
2069 Coldwater Canyon Drive, Los Angeles

Although James Cagney is best known for his gangster roles in such films as *Public Enemy* (1931), he liked to say that he was just a hoofer at heart. In fact, Cagney starred in several musicals that featured his dancing skills, most notably *Footlight Parade* (1933) and *Yankee Doodle Dandy* (1942), for which he won the Oscar for Best Actor. He also starred in *Mister Roberts* (1955) and *Man of a Thousand Faces* (1957).

1315½ North Hayworth Avenue: Shortly after arriving in Hollywood from New York, Cagney rented a bungalow in this West Hollywood court-yard complex.

2069 Coldwater Canyon Drive: Cagney's Cold-water Canyon house was as unpretentious as its owner. Built in 1939, the six-room house on this property was tiny by Hollywood-star stan-dards. The house featured a warm, rustic interior. Cagney lived here for many years beginning in the early 1940s.

Michael Caine (1933–)
315 Trousdale Place, Beverly Hills

Michael Caine gained international acclaim after he starred in two popular British movies, *The Ipcress File* (1965) and *Alfie* (1966). Caine, who likes to point out that he's not above choosing a part for the money or the filming location, scored big in the second half of his career with *The Man Who Would be King* (1975), *Educating Rita* (1983), and his two Oscar-winning efforts—*Hannah and Her Sisters* (1986) and *Cider House Rules* (1999).

Caine resided in this light beige, multi-columned house from 1991 to 1995. In his memoir, Caine explained how Beverly Hills surprised him. "I always thought of Beverly Hills as a place that consisted of nothing but glamour, but was surprised to find ordinary amenities, too," he wrote. "There used to be a hardware store right on Beverly Drive…I once saw Fred Astaire buying sandpaper and Danny Kaye buying one light bulb."

Rory Calhoun (1922–1999)
901 North Bedford Drive, Beverly Hills

A former lumberjack and truck driver, Rory Calhoun was discovered in 1943 by Western star Alan Ladd when the two crossed paths while riding horses in the Hollywood Hills. Calhoun became known primarily for his roles in the adventure and Western fare that Hollywood cranked out from the 1940s to the mid-1960s, including *Red Sundown* (1956) and *Ride Out*

for Revenge (1957). Among Calhoun's forays outside of that genre was his supporting role in *How to Marry a Millionaire* (1953).

Calhoun lived in this Mediterranean-style house during the 1960s. He also owned a ranch near Ojai.

Michael Caine
315 Trousdale Place, Beverly Hills

Jim Carrey (1962–)
615 North Tigertail Road, Brentwood

Jim Carrey's trademark elastic face and bizarre humor are on display in movies such as *Ace Ventura: Pet Detective* (1994), *The Mask* (1994) and *Liar, Liar* (1997). But many critics say Carrey's best performances have been in more serious fare, including *The Truman Show* (1998) and *Man on the Moon*

(1999). Before he became a movie star, Carrey was the opening act for comedian Rodney Dangerfield, and a cast member of the ground-breaking TV show *In Living Color* (1990–1993).

Carrey owned this Brentwood estate in the 1990s. He moved on to Venice, then bought a house in Malibu in 2003. Meanwhile, his old Brentwood house has undergone extensive renovations.

Dana Carvey (1955–)
17333 Rancho Street, Encino

Dana Carvey earned legions of fans in the early 1990s for his impersonations of George Bush, Sr., and Ross Perot during his 1986–1993 tenure on the TV show *Saturday Night Live*, and later on *The Dana Carvey Show* (1996). He showed up in small movie roles in the 1980s, including the waiter who per-

forms mime in *This Is Spinal Tap* (1984). Carvey later starred in *Wayne's World* (1992) and its sequel *Wayne's World 2* (1993).

Carvey owned this Encino property from 1987 to 1995, the years during which he was taping *Saturday Night Live* in New York.

Marge Champion (1919–)
Gower Champion (1921–1980)
7647 Woodrow Wilson Drive, Hollywood Hills

Marge and Gower Champion entertained moviegoers not by acting, but by dancing. After their screen debut in *Show Boat* (1951), the Champions stepped lightly in several movies, including *Lovely to Look At* (1952) and *Everything I Have Is Yours* (1952). Prior to teaming with Gower, Marge had a bit part in the Fred Astaire and Ginger Rogers film *The Story of Vernon and Irene Castle* (1939).

In the 1950s, the Champions lived in the house located at the end of a long driveway that curves up to the house.

Jeff Chandler (1918–1961)
1152 San Ysidro Drive, Beverly Hills

The lanky, prematurely gray-haired Jeff Chandler appeared in several Westerns and adventure movies before graduating to leading-man roles in such movies as *Return to Peyton Place* (1961). His death at age 42 (from blood poisoning following back surgery) was ruled a case of medical malpractice.

A brick walkway leads to the dark-green front door of this house, where Chandler lived in the 1950s.

❖

Lon Chaney (1883–1930)
Regent Beverly Wilshire Hotel
9500 Wilshire Boulevard, Beverly Hills

Lon Chaney, "The Man of a Thousand Faces," was an early innovator of movie make-up techniques. He also gained notoriety for infusing humanity into grotesque characters such as Quasimoto in *The Hunchback of Notre Dame* (1923). After that success, Chaney starred in such movies as *He Who Gets Slapped* (1924) and *The Phantom of the Opera* (1925).

Chaney could be called "the man with a thousand houses." He lived in numerous different homes during his Hollywood career, but the only ones which are believed to have survived are his cabin in the eastern Sierras and his final residence, The Beverly Wilshire Hotel (today known as the Regent Beverly Wilshire). Chaney died of lung cancer while he and his family were living in the hotel, waiting for their new Beverly Hills house to be built.

Lon Chaney, Jr. (1906–1973)
1856 Bel Air Road, Bel Air

Although his father, Lon Chaney, discouraged his son from becoming an actor, the younger Chaney followed his father into horror-films. Lon Chaney, Jr., starred in *The Wolf Man* (1941) and re-created his Wolf Man character in several more movies, including *Frankenstein Meets the Wolf Man* (1943) and *Abbott & Costello Meet Frankenstein* (1948).

It's a steep and winding 2½-mile drive from the elegant gate at Bel Air's Sunset and Beverly Glen entrance, to this brick-front house. Chaney lived here in the 1950s.

Charlie Chaplin (1889–1977)
6147 Temple Hill Drive, Hollywood Hills
1085 Summit Drive, Beverly Hills

To most moviegoers, Charlie Chaplin's name is synonymous with The Little Tramp—the clever, rag-tag character he played in scores of shorts and features from the mid-teens through the early 1930s. Among Chaplin's many masterpieces are *The Kid* (1921), *The Gold Rush* (1925) and *City Lights* (1931). Chaplin moved to Switzerland in the early 1950s, when the U.S. government began questioning his political leanings and income tax returns. In 1972, he returned to the United States just long enough to receive an honorary Oscar for his contributions to filmmaking.

6147 Temple Hill Drive: In the early 1920s, Chaplin rented this East Indian-style house in a region of Hollywood known as Hollywood Dell.

1085 Summit Drive: Douglas Fairbanks and Mary Pickford helped Chaplin pick the site of this Beverly Hills estate. Construction began in 1922, and took several years. The house has been called "The Breakaway House" because Chaplin hired studio carpenters for part of the construction. It's on 6 acres, just below Pickfair. A serious tennis player, Chaplin would play with friends, like tennis pro Bill Tilden, on the estate's tennis court. Pola Negri, who was involved with Chaplin when the house was being built, selected many of the plants and trees.

Charley Chase (1893–1940)
182 North Tigertail Road, Brentwood

Audiences considered Charley Chase's fast-paced, two-reel comedies to be among the funniest shorts during the silent era. In 1924 alone, he made 28 films for Hal Roach Studios, often playing a henpecked or straying husband in films with titles like *Why Husbands Go Mad* (1924) and *The Way of All Pants* (1927).

After Chase purchased this Mediterranean-style Brentwood house in 1929, he made extensive renovations. Several years earlier, Chase lived on Highland Avenue near the site of today's Hollywood Bowl.

Ruth Chatterton (1893–1961)
704 North Palm Drive, Beverly Hills

Ruth Chatterton was a 35-year-old stage actress in Los Angeles when she was discovered by film star Emil Jannings. Chatterton starred in the popular *Madam X* (1929), but she is better known for her supporting roles in such later films as *The Rich are Always with Us* (1932), one of several movies Chatterton made with husband George Brent. In *Dodsworth* (1936), she played the difficult wife of Walter Huston.

Chatterton and her husband, actor George Brent, lived in this Palm Drive house during the period in which she co-starred in *Dodsworth*, giving what many consider to be her best performance.

Virginia Cherrill (1908–1996)
Mi Casa Apartments
1400–1414 North Havenhurst Drive
West Hollywood

Her movie career may have lasted just six years, but Virginia Cherrill's turn as the blind flower girl in Charlie Chaplin's 1931 silent film, *City Lights,* guarantees her a place among the celluloid immortals. Cherrill was a young socialite who had toyed with acting when Chaplin hired her after an exhaustive search for the right actress to play the role. Although she and Chaplin exhibit a striking

chemistry in the film, it was a different story behind the scenes. Years later, Cherrill said, "I never liked Charlie and he never liked me."

Cherrill resided here with her husband, Cary Grant, in 1934, during their brief marriage. After they divorced, Grant moved into the apartment next door. At the time that Grant and Cherrill lived here, it was called the Ronda Apartments.

Ruth Clifford (1900–1998)
720 North Foothill Road, Beverly Hills

Ruth Clifford had a busy career in silent movies, appearing in such hits as *Abraham Lincoln* (1924). John Ford cast her in several movies, including *Wagon Master* (1950). Clifford can also been seen in *Funny Girl* (1968) as Barbra Streisand's housekeeper.

Clifford's husband, real estate magnet J.A. Cornelius, built this home in 1924, the year they were married. Conrad Veidt lived here a few years later.

George Clooney (1961–)
11655 Laurelcrest Drive, Studio City

George Clooney had already won over TV audiences as the impetuous pediatrician in the TV series *ER*, when he landed his first major movie role starring opposite Michelle Pfeiffer in *One Fine Day* (1996). Clooney followed that with several box office hits, including *Out of Sight* (1998) and *Ocean's Eleven* (2001). Clooney, who was named "Sexiest Man Alive" by *People* magazine in 1997, is the nephew of the late singer and actress Rosemary Clooney.

Clooney could look out over the San Fernando Valley from this Studio City hillside house he bought in 1990. He sold the house in 1997, the same year in which he slipped into his Batman tights to star in *Batman and Robin*.

Rosemary Clooney (1928–2002)
1019 North Roxbury Drive, Beverly Hills

Singer Rosemary Clooney was a chart-topping singer when she signed on for her first movie, *The Stars Are Singing* (1953). The next year she appeared in the holiday favorite *White Christmas* (1954), co-starring Bing Crosby, Danny Kaye and Vera Ellyn.

Built in 1928, Clooney's long-time Beverly Hills home sits on an acre of land, and includes a pool, a tennis court and a guest-house. Composer George Gershwin owned this house at one time.

Lee J. Cobb (1911–1976)
605 North Arden Drive, Beverly Hills

Lee J. Cobb's cranky on-screen manner helped win him the role of William Holden's father in *Golden Boy* (1939), even though Cobb was only nine years older than Holden. In 1953, Cobb testified before the House Un-American Activities Committee that 20 of his colleagues were Communists. Although movie roles became scarce after that, he played several memorable parts, including the tough labor leader in *On the Waterfront* (1954), a nightmare juror in *12 Angry Men* (1957), and the confused spy in *Our Man Flint* (1966) and *In Like Flint* (1967).

Cobb lived here during the 1950s, before his career took a tailspin. While recuperating from a heart attack in 1955, Cobb stayed at Frank Sinatra's Palm Springs house, and then moved into a Los Angeles apartment that was paid for by Sinatra.

Lee J. Cobb
605 North Arden Drive, Beverly Hills

Charles Coburn (1877–1961)
7935 Hollywood Boulevard, Hollywood

Heavy-set and often sporting a monocle, Charles Coburn showed up in colorful supporting roles from the 1930s through the 1950s. He won an Academy Award for Best Supporting Actor for his portrayal of the cupid who unites Jean Arthur and Joel McCrea in *The More the Merrier* (1943). In the 1950s, Coburn played elderly gents who were smitten with Marilyn Monroe in *Monkey Business* (1952) and *Gentlemen Prefer Blondes* (1953).

Coburn's home in the 1940s was this Spanish-style house with a distinctive octagonal tower. The house stands near the intersection of Laurel Canyon and Hollywood Boulevard.

James Coburn (1928–2002)
1146 Tower Road, Beverly Hills

James Coburn's send-up of James Bond in *Our Man Flint* (1966) and *In Like Flint* (1967) brought him fame in the mid-1960s, but those spy spoofs weren't his first significant films. Coburn was a cohort of Steve McQueen in *The Magnificent Seven* (1960) and *The Great Escape* (1963). More than 30 years later, Coburn won the Academy Award for Best Supporting Actor for his performance as Nick Nolte's spiteful father in *Affliction* (1998).

Coburn's Spanish Colonial Revival house overlooks Beverly Hills. When Coburn sold it in the late 1980s, it had 40 rooms.

Charles Coburn
7935 Hollywood Boulevard, Hollywood

Lew Cody (1884–1934)
609 North Maple Drive, Beverly Hills

Lew Cody began his theatrical career managing theatre stock companies. He first appeared on the screen in 1915, and went on to become one of the silent screen's

most debonair and devilish leading men. Among Cody's most notable films were *Rupert of Hentzau* (1923) and *Hello Frisco* (1924).

Cody was so fond of antiques, some said that his house resembled a museum. Mabel Normand moved into this house after she married Cody in 1926. The couple liked to ask their guests to carve their names on the front door before entering.

Claudette Colbert (1903–1996)
615 North Faring Road, Holmby Hills

The likeable Claudette Colbert was equally at home in melodramas and comedies during her 34-year screen career. Colbert's light touch as an heiress on

the run, opposite Clark Gable in *It Happened One Night* (1934), earned her the Best Actress Academy Award. Colbert's other popular pictures include *Imitation of Life* (1934) and *The Palm Beach Story* (1942).

In 1935, Colbert commissioned Lloyd Wright to design this house. Colbert's mansion was only the second house on the street. In 1961, she left Hollywood and settled in Barbados where she renovated a plantation house on the edge of the Caribbean.

Betty Compson (1897–1974)
901 North Camden Drive, Beverly Hills

Betty Compson starred in Al Christie silent comedies before appearing with Lon Chaney in the drama *The Miracle Man* (1919). She followed a successful career in silents with smaller roles in talk-

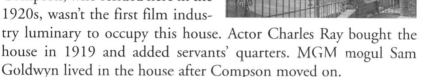

ing pictures. These include *Strange Cargo* (1940) with Clark Gable and Joan Crawford, and the Alfred Hitchcock thriller, *Mr. and Mrs. Smith* (1941).

Compson, who resided here in the 1920s, wasn't the first film indus-
try luminary to occupy this house. Actor Charles Ray bought the house in 1919 and added servants' quarters. MGM mogul Sam Goldwyn lived in the house after Compson moved on.

Richard Conte (1910–1975)
1119 San Ysidro Drive, Beverly Hills

Richard Conte can be seen in supporting roles in scores of mysteries and crime dramas during the 1950s, including *Call Northside 777* (1948) and *House of Strangers* (1949). He is also memorable in a lighter role, that of Judy Holliday's husband in *Full of Life* (1957). Three years before he died, Conte played Barzini, a Corleone family rival in *The Godfather* (1972).

Conte lived in this Mediterranean-style home during the 1950s.

Gary Cooper (1901–1961)
7511 Franklin Avenue, Hollywood
200 Baroda Drive, Holmby Hills

From *Wings* (1927) to *High Noon* (1952) to *Love in the Afternoon* (1957), Gary Cooper's understated acting style set him apart from other leading men of his era. Cooper earned Best Actor Oscars for *Sergeant York* (1941) and *High Noon.*

7511 Franklin Avenue: While trying his hand at acting in the mid 1920s, Cooper lived with his parents in this Hollywood house. A few years later he moved two miles east to the Castle Argyle apartments.

200 Baroda Drive: In 1954, Cooper built his dream house—a contemporary, one-story home of glass, redwood and Palos Verdes stone that is barely visible from the street. In the 1950s, Cooper said of the house, "It was so advanced in outline, that we sometimes wonder if we're in the year 2000."

Jackie Cooper (1922–)
702 North Crescent Drive, Beverly Hills

Jackie Cooper, who had a knack for crying on cue as a child actor, appeared in more than a dozen Our Gang comedy shorts. His performance in his first feature film, *Skippy* (1931), led to a nomination for the Best Actor Oscar.

Cooper was the youngest person to be nominated for that award. Cooper's next project was co-starring with Wallace Beery in *The Champ* (1931). He appeared in several more movies before turning to television. He later became an award-winning director.

Cooper lived here in the mid-1930s. As a youngster, he assumed it was normal to live in a house with a swimming pool—until he went to Beverly Hills High School. Suddenly he had a horde of friends at school. He came to realize that it was his swimming pool—not his movie-star status—that made him so popular.

Miriam Cooper (1894–1976)
626 South Plymouth Boulevard, Los Angeles

In her brief film career, Miriam Cooper managed to appear in two historic films, *The Birth of a Nation* (1915) and *Intolerance* (1916). After she married director Raoul Walsh in 1916, Cooper starred in several films directed by Walsh.

In 1924, Cooper and Walsh bought this classic Mediterranean-style house near Hancock Park. Walsh also owned a ranch in Encino, which he later sold to Clark Gable.

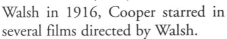

Lou Costello (1906–1959)
4124 Longridge Avenue, Sherman Oaks

Lou Costello was the stubby, child-like member of the famed Abbott & Costello comedy team. Before joining forces with Bud Abbott, Costello was a studio carpenter and a vaudeville performer. He and Abbott made 38 movies together between 1940 and 1956, and starred in two TV series from 1951–1954. Like his partner, Costello earned producer credits on several of their movies.

Costello paid $13,500 for this San Fernando Valley house in the 1940s. The house was on one acre of land. Costello expanded the house and designed a family flag that flew in front of the house.

Joseph Cotten (1905–1994)
17800 Tramonto Drive, Pacific Palisades

Joseph Cotten was a member of the Mercury Theater ensemble which Orson Welles brought to Hollywood from New York. Cotten co-starred in Welles' *Citizen Kane* (1941) as Kane's best friend, and *The Magnificent Ambersons* (1942) as Dolores Costello's gentleman friend. He also played the psychopathic uncle in Alfred Hitchcock's *Shadow of a Doubt* (1943), and the heroic investigator in *Gaslight* (1944).

Cotten bought this house before he married actress Patricia Medina in 1960. Shortly after they married, they embarked on an extensive remodeling project that involved installing an outdoor swimming pool into the space that had previously been a drawing room overlooking the ocean. Cotten helped the workmen finish the pool's deck.

Joseph Cotten
17800 Tramonto Drive, Pacific Palisades

Broderick Crawford (1911–1986)
Argyle Hotel
8358 West Sunset Boulevard, West Hollywood

Six years before he began starring in the TV series *Highway Patrol* (1955–1959), Broderick Crawford collected an Academy Award for Best Actor for his portrayal of a politician who descends into a life of corruption in *All the King's Men* (1949). The movie also won Best Picture in 1949. Crawford followed that success by playing Judy Holliday's millionaire boyfriend in *Born Yesterday* (1950).

In the 1950s, Crawford lived in what is now called the Argyle Hotel. At the time, the Art Deco building was known as the Sunset Tower. Many actors, including Paulette Goddard and John Wayne, have lived at the Sunset Tower over the years.

Joan Crawford (1904–1977)
Hotel West End
3927 Van Buren Place, Culver CIty
426 North Bristol Avenue, Brentwood

Square-jawed Joan Crawford was one of the queens of the Hollywood melodrama. She won an Academy Award for Best Actress for her performance as the humorless, fretting mother in *Mildred Pierce* (1945). Crawford's other important roles include a flighty flapper in *Our Dancing Daughters* (1928), and emotionally fragile women in *Grand Hotel* (1932) and *What Ever Happened to Baby Jane* (1962).

Hotel West End: The Hotel Washington in Culver City, now called Hotel West End, was Crawford's first home when she arrived in California in the mid-1920s. She rented a room here to be close to the MGM studios.

426 North Bristol Avenue: In 1928, when *Our Dancing Daughters* hit the screen, Louis B. Mayer lent Crawford $40,000 so she could buy this house in Brentwood. After Crawford's daughter, Christina Crawford, wrote a memoir about her troubled childhood, the Bristol Avenue house became known as the "Mommie Dearest House." Actor Donald O'Connor later bought the house.

Bing Crosby (1903–1977)
4326 Forman Avenue, Toluca Lake

Bing Crosby debuted on the screen as a singer with The Paul Whiteman Orchestra in the early talkie *King of Jazz* (1930). Crosby was later cast in supporting roles in such movies as *Holiday Inn* (1942), where he introduced Irving Berlin's song, "White Christmas." In the 1940s, Crosby teamed with

Bob Hope and Dorothy Lamour for a series of "Road" pictures. In the late 1940s, Crosby helped pioneer the use of magnetic tape to pre-record radio shows.

After his 1930 marriage to actress Dix Lee, Crosby built this house in Toluca Lake. The home's interiors were designed by Harold Grieve, a decorator who was popular among movie stars of the era. Another Toluca Lake house Crosby built burned to the ground in 1943, a result of a short circuit in the home's Christmas lights.

Tom Cruise (1962–)
1525 Sorrento Drive, Pacific Palisades

Since making his film debut in *Endless Love* (1981), Tom Cruise has become one of Hollywood's favorite leading men, and one of the highest-paid stars in history. He has been featured in such hit films as *Rain Man* (1988),

Jerry McGuire (1996) and *Mission Impossible* (1996).

Cruise and his wife, Nicole Kidman, lived in the 7,597-square-foot house on this Pacific Palisades estate from the early 1990s until their divorce in 2001.

Billy Crystal (1947–)
860 Chautauqua Boulevard, Pacific Palisades

Billy Crystal has starred in comedies such as *City Slickers* (1991) and *Analyze This* (1999). He has also blended drama with comedy in *When Harry Met Sally* (1989) and *Mr. Saturday Night* (1992).

Crystal has produced and directed several movies, and earned three Emmy Awards for his skillful hosting of Academy Awards shows.

A charming white fence guards a 4,200-square-foot house on this property which Crystal has owned since the 1980s. On a side note, the living room of Crystal's childhood house on Long Island served as his first stage. He entertained his relatives by impersonating them. They paid him in dimes.

Robert Cummings (1908–1990)
1060 Laurel Way, Beverly Hills

There was a casual air about Robert Cummings, whether he played a mild-mannered medical student or a fast-talking ladies man. After being paired with Deanna Durbin for several light, coming-of-age comedies, Cummings landed meatier roles in such movies as *The Devil and Miss Jones* (1941), *Kings Row* (1942) and *Dial M for Murder* (1954). In the 1950s and 1960s, Cummings starred in, and often directed, *The Bob Cummings Show* and *Love That Bob* (1955–1959 and 1961–1962).

Cummings lived in this Beverly Hills house during the 1950s when he was appearing in movies and on TV.

Tony Curtis (1925–)
1178 Loma Linda Drive, Beverly Hills

Tony Curtis—curly-haired and movie-star handsome—worked in dozens of movies during the 1950s before rising to stardom with his performance as the slimy press agent in *Sweet Smell of Success* (1957). Curtis' other box office hits include *The Defiant Ones* (1958), the blockbuster comedy *Some Like It Hot* (1959) and *The Great Race* (1965).

Curtis lived here in the 1960s. As a young actor during the late 1940s, he roomed with Burt Lancaster in Hollywood.

Dorothy Dandridge (1923–1965)
8430 Franklin Avenue, Hollywood Hills

In one of her first movie roles, Dorothy Dandridge appeared as a singer in the Marx Brothers' classic, *A Day at the Races* (1937). After some time away from the screen to perform in nightclubs, Dandridge returned to co-star with Harry Belafonte in three movies, including *Carmen Jones* (1954). Her portrayal of the cold-hearted title character led to a nomination for the Best Actress Oscar. Five years later, Dandridge starred opposite Sidney Poitier in George and Ira Gershwin's *Porgy and Bess* (1959).

During the 1950s, Dandridge lived in this house overlooking Hollywood. After filing for bankruptcy in the early 1960s, she gave up the house and rented an apartment on Fountain Avenue in West Hollywood.

Dorothy Dandridge
8430 Franklin Avenue, Hollywood Hills

Karl Dane (1886–1934)
520 North Elm Drive, Beverly Hills

Karl Dane's acting career began as a teenager on a Copenhagen stage. After serving as one of the Danish Flying Corps' first pilots, he played Slim in the World War I drama *The Big Parade* (1925), and went on to win comic roles in *The Son of the Sheik* (1926) and *The Scarlet Letter* (1926). After

being told that his Danish accent was too heavy for sound pictures, he found himself working menial jobs, at one point selling hot dogs outside of MGM studios where he had once been a star. Dane was so despondent over his fate that he committed suicide at the age of 48.

Dane lived here during the height of his career. He later moved to a Fairfax-area apartment. He fatally shot himself there, surrounded by newspaper clippings from his former life as a movie star.

Bebe Daniels (1901–1971)
1022 Palisades Beach Road, Santa Monica

Babe Daniels appeared in Harold Lloyd shorts before graduating to substantial roles in such dramas as Rudolph Valentino's *Monsieur Beaucaire* (1924). She later performed on British radio programs.

In the 1920s, Daniels, her mother and grandmother so enjoyed spending weekends in Santa Monica, they built this beachfront house and lived here full-time. Daniels sold the house in 1948.

Marion Davies (1897–1961)
415 Palisades Beach Road, Santa Monica
1700 Lexington Place, Beverly Hills

Although media millionaire William Randolph Hearst tried to steer his lover, Marion Davies, toward dramatic film roles early in her career, it was Davies' impressive comedic talent that garnered her legions of fans. Her most popular films include *The Patsy* (1928), *Show People* (1928) and *Cain and Mabel* (1936).

415 Palisades Beach Road: All that is left of Davies' legendary Santa Monica estate is the servants' wing on the north side of the original property (the building on the far right). Hearst built the estate for Davies in 1928. It had 110 rooms and could accommodate 2,000 guests.

1700 Lexington Place: Davies was famous for her costume parties. She recalled of one particular party in her memoir: "At the Lexington Rd. house we had a baby party, and people you didn't know could get in. A character with a big head and a mask came in wearing a diaper…we thought he was a prowler, but nothing was missing. In fact, something was added. There was a gun left in the hall."

Bette Davis (1908–1989)
Colonial House
1416 North Havenhurst Drive, West Hollywood

Bette Davis' early signature roles included the spoiled Julie Marsden in *Jezebel* (1938) and the ruthless Regina Giddens in *The Little Foxes* (1941). A decade later Davis gave one of her most admired performances when she starred as the complex Margo Channing in *All About Eve* (1950). She won Best Actress Oscars for *Dangerous* (1935) and *Jezebel.*

Davis lived at the posh Colonial House during the last several years of her life. Other actors who have lived at the Colonial House include William Powell and Carole Lombard, who took an apartment after they married. Davis owned houses in Toluca Lake and Bel Air at different points of her career. In June 1957, while moving into a rented Brentwood house she opened a door that she thought led to a closet, but it actually went to the basement. She fell down 14 stairs and broke her back.

Sammy Davis, Jr. (1925–1990)
1151 Summit Drive, Beverly Hills

Sammy Davis, Jr., broke into show business as a pint-sized member of the song-and-dance stage act started by his father and uncle. Hollywood soon cast him in two short films. Davis' first credited role as an adult was opposite Eartha Kitt in *Anna Lucasta* (1958). He also played Sportin' Life in

Porgy and Bess (1959) and co-starred in several "Rat Pack" movies with Frank Sinatra.

Davis lived on this Beverly Hills estate from the early 1970s until his death. The estate included a 10,900-square-foot mansion, and a separate building which served as his gourmet kitchen.

Bette Davis
Colonial House, 1416 North Havenhurst Drive, West Hollywood

❖

Doris Day (1924–)
713 North Crescent Drive, Beverly Hills

Doris Day sang with the Bob Crosby and Les Brown bands before being cast in a small part in her first movie, *Romance on the High Seas* (1948). Day proved to be skilled at light comedy in movies such as *Pajama Game* (1957), *Pillow Talk* (1959) and *The Thrill of It All* (1963). She also garnered good reviews for dramatic performances in such movies as *The Man Who Knew Too Much* (1956).

Day moved into this house in the early 1960s and stayed for more than two decades. When it came to decorating the house, Day's priority was comfort. "My motto is 'Better to please the fanny than the eye,'" she once said. During the late-1940s, Day lived in a Los Angeles trailer park with her second husband and young son.

Laraine Day (1917–)
925 North Alpine Drive, Beverly Hills

Laraine Day earned a following as Nurse Lamont in seven *Dr. Kildare* movies made between 1939 and 1941. She also starred in Alfred Hitchcock's *Foreign Correspondent* (1940), and opposite Cary Grant in *Mr. Lucky* (1943). While married to New York Giants manager Leo Durocher, Day became known as "The First Lady of Baseball."

Day and Durocher, married from 1947 to 1960, divided their time between a New York home and this Beverly Hills house.

James Dean (1931–1955)
601 Gayley Avenue, Westwood

James Dean's edgy performances in *East of Eden* (1955), *Rebel Without a Cause* (1955) and *Giant* (1956) continue to resonate with audiences. Dean died at the age of 24 when his Porsche smashed into a pole in central California. Dean played the lead in three films and earned Academy Award nominations for two, *East of Eden* and *Giant*.

While attending UCLA in the late 1940s, Dean lived in this Sigma Nu fraternity house near the Westwood campus. After he became a star, Dean bought a house in Encino where locals remember that Dean liked to race his car down Ventura Boulevard.

Dolores Del Rio (1905–1983)
757 Kingman Avenue, Santa Monica

Dolores Del Rio, who hailed from a wealthy Mexican family, had important roles in such silent films has *What Price Glory* (1926) and *Resurrection* (1927).

Del Rio can also be seen singing and dancing in *Flying Down to Rio* (1933) and *Wonder Bar* (1934). During the 1940s and 1950s, Del Rio made most of her movies in Mexico.

Shortly after Del Rio married MGM art director Cedric Gibbons in 1930, he began designing this Art Moderne-style house. The grounds included a multi-level garden and a tennis court with a gallery area for spectators. Inside were sleek furnishings and mirrored walls. Gibbons, who designed the Academy Award's Oscar statuette, won 12 Oscars himself.

William Demarest (1892–1983)
3310 Wonder View Plaza, Los Angeles

William Demarest was a grouchy presence in movies from the 1930s through the 1970s. He was especially memorable in such comedies as *Christmas in July* (1940), *The Lady Eve* (1941) and *The Miracle of Morgan's Creek* (1944). Demarest later co-starred as Uncle Charlie on the *My Three Sons* TV series (1965–1972).

Demarest's home during the 1940s is just off the Cahuenga Pass and less than a mile from Lake Hollywood Reservoir and Mulholland Dam.

Danny DeVito (1944–)
2424 Nottingham Avenue, Los Feliz

Short, balding Danny DeVito has been a featured character actor in movies ranging from *One Flew Over the Cuckoo's Nest* (1975) to *L.A. Confidential* (1997). DeVito also starred in, and directed, *War of the Roses* (1989) and *Throw Momma from the Train* (1987).

This house, where DeVito lived in the 1980s and 1990s, is located in Los Feliz, a tony hillside community just north of Hollywood. Los Feliz was home to many of Hollywood's early pioneers and stars, including director Cecil B. DeMille and actor W.C. Fields.

Marlene Dietrich (1901–1992)
822 North Roxbury Drive, Beverly Hills

Thanks to Marlene Dietrich's smoky voice, laconic manner and movies that today are considered campy, she has become more famous as a cult figure than an actress. Her early films, including *Shanghai Express* (1932) and *Blonde Venus* (1932), were box-office hits but didn't wow the critics. Dietrich finally won them over toward the end of her movie career when she played the widow of a Nazi officer in *Judgment at Nuremberg* (1961).

When Dietrich rented this Roxbury Drive house in the early 1930s, she had bars installed on the windows after receiving a threatening unsigned note. The house was built in 1928 and is one of the early Moderne-style houses in Beverly Hills.

Richard Dix (1894–1949)
1111 Calle Vista Drive, Beverly Hills

Richard Dix was a consummate "man's man" on screen, portraying football players, aerobatic pilots and Western heroes. His best-known role may be that of the crazed captain in *The Ghost Ship* (1943). Among his other high-profile films were *The Ten Commandments* (1923) and *Cimarron* (1931).

This estate, where Dix luxuriated during the 1930s and 1940s, commands a hillside overlooking Sunset Boulevard. (This view of the house is from Doheny Road.)

Marlene Dietrich
822 North Roxbury Drive, Beverly Hills

Brian Donlevy (1901–1972)
10401 Wilshire Boulevard, Los Angeles

Brian Donlevy played characters to be reckoned with in such movies as *Barbary Coast* (1935) and *Jesse James* (1939). He showed his humorous side in Preston Sturges' *The Great McGinty* (1940). Away from the screen, Donlevy

published a book of poetry entitled *Leaves in the Wind,* using the pen name "Porter Down."

In the 1950s, Donlevy lived in this apartment building along the Wilshire Corridor near Beverly Glen. He retired to Palm Springs in 1969.

Kirk Douglas (1916–)
707 North Canon Drive, Beverly Hills

Rugged, cleft-chinned Kirk Douglas literally came out swinging in the role that made him a star, that of a self-centered boxer in *Champion* (1949). He went on to portray other troubled, head-strong men in such movies as *Young Man with a Horn* (1950), and played romantic leading men in movies

such as *Strangers When We Meet* (1960). At age 70 he joined Burt Lancaster in *Tough Guys* (1986).

Douglas lived in this spacious Mediterranean-style house for about 20 years. After relocating to a smaller house in the late 1970s, Douglas commented that this mansion was never his dream house. "The day we moved out of that house neither my wife nor I had any emotional feelings about it. It was never *our* house," he said.

Billie Dove (1901–1998)
719 Amalfi Drive, Pacific Palisades

The fan magazines dubbed Billie Dove "The American Beauty" after she starred in the 1927 movie of the same name. Dove also has the distinction of co-starring in two of the earliest Technicolor feature-length films, *Wanderer of the Wasteland* (1924), directed by her husband, Irvin Willat, and the Douglas Fairbanks hit, *The Black Pirate* (1926).

Dove built this hacienda-style house in the Pacific Palisades in the early 1930s.

Marie Dressler (1869–1934)
623 North Bedford Drive, Beverly Hills

Marie Dressler's first film, *Tillie's Punctured Romance* (1914), was America's first feature-length comedy. The heavy-set Dressler went on to co-star in more silent comedies and continued in talkies, stealing the show in such movies as *Anna Christie* (1930), *Min and Bill* (1930) and *Dinner at Eight* (1933).

Dressler bought this Federal-style house in the early 1930s. The many homey touches in the house included items she bought at second-hand stores and auctions. Dressler once said, "Ever since I can remember I've been saving things to go into a house."

Richard Dreyfuss (1947–)
2809 Nichols Canyon Road, Hollywood Hills

Part everyman, part eccentric, Richard Dreyfuss has won praise for his performances, ranging from a sensitive teen in *American Graffiti* (1973), to a UFO enthusiast in *Close Encounters of the Third Kind* (1977), to the hapless psychiatrist in *What About Bob?* (1991). Dreyfuss won the Academy Award for Best Actor for his performance in *The Goodbye Girl* (1977).

Dreyfuss bought this Nichols Canyon property in 1983 and sold it in the mid-1990s. Nichols Canyon Road starts at the north end of Hollywood Boulevard and winds through rural territory into the Hollywood Hills.

Marie Dressler
623 North Bedford Drive, Beverly Hills

Faye Dunaway (1941–)
1435 Lindacrest Drive, Los Angeles

Faye Dunaway starred in such blockbusters as *Bonnie and Clyde* (1967), *Chinatown* (1974) and *Network* (1976), which have become classics in the eyes of many critics. Dunaway was honored with the Academy Award for Best Actress for her portrayal of the high-strung TV news director in *Network*.

Dunaway purchased this corner house in the 1990s. There are steps leading from Lindacrest to a front lawn that is made very private by trees and hedges. Dunaway previously lived in New York.

Jimmy Durante (1893–1980)
511 North Beverly Drive, Beverly Hills

Jimmy Durante's comic character—a little guy who growled out songs and joked about his prominent nose—appeared in more than 40 movies, from 1930's *Road House Nights* to his grand finale in 1963, *It's a Mad Mad Mad Mad World*. He teamed briefly with Buster Keaton in the early talkie days, then went on to supporting roles in several movies.

Durante lived in this low-slung Beverly Drive house for many years. During the 1960s, Durante and his family rented a summer house in the seaside community of Del Mar, 112 miles south of Beverly Hills. He was so popular in Del Mar that the city named a street after him. In 1931, when Durante first came west to work in movies, he rented a tiny bungalow in Pasadena.

Jimmy Durante
511 North Beverly Drive, Beverly Hills

Deanna Durbin (1921–)
7922 Hollywood Boulevard, Hollywood

Deanna Durbin's polished soprano singing voice and clean-cut beauty, made her one of the top teenage stars during the 1930s. She received a special juvenile

Academy Award in 1938. A year later, she earned her first star billing in *Three Smart Girls Grow Up* (1939), which was a sequel to her debut feature, *Three Smart Girls* (1936). She retired from show business in 1948.

Durbin lived in this house, on the west end of Hollywood Boulevard, in the early 1940s when she was married to her first husband, studio executive Vaughn Paul. After leaving Hollywood, she lived for many years in Paris, France with her third husband, director Charles David.

Dan Duryea (1907–1968)
7621 Mulholland Drive, Hollywood Hills

Dan Duryea played unsavory characters in some of the top box-office hits of Hollywood's golden age. Duryea reprised his Broadway role as the greedy young Leo

Hubbard in *The Little Foxes* for the 1941 movie version starring Bette Davis. He also played a world-weary sportswriter in *Pride of the Yankees* (1942) with Gary Cooper.

This classic Spanish-style house hails from the 1920s and overlooks the San Fernando Valley. Duryea lived here in the 1950s.

Ann Dvorak (1911–1979)
232 South New Hampshire Avenue
Los Angeles

After making 20 movies, first as a child actress and then as a chorus girl, Ann Dvorak landed her first credited role in *Sky Devils* (1932). Although true stardom eluded her, Dvorak's knack for playing troubled women made her a favorite for gangster films and melodramas such as *Scarface* (1932) and *Three on a Match* (1932).

Dvorak lived in this Mediterranean-style house in the Westlake area of Los Angeles during the mid-1930s. After she retired from moviemaking in 1951, Dvorak and her third husband, TV producer Nicholas Wade, lived in Malibu and Honolulu.

Clint Eastwood (1930–)
427 South Oakhurst Street, Beverly Hills

The studios discovered Clint Eastwood's star power when he made *A Fistful of Dollars* (1967) and its sequels. He was suddenly in demand for Westerns and action movies, including *Paint Your Wagon* (1969) and *Dirty Harry* (1971). Eastwood produced, directed and starred in *Unforgiven* (1992), a Western that won the Academy Award for Best Picture.

While managing his fledgling movie career during the 1950s, Eastwood was also managing this apartment building. This was also the first home where Eastwood and his wife, Maggie, lived after they married in 1953.

Buddy Ebsen (1908–2003)
530 South Bay Front, Balboa Island

Long before he was identified by his TV characters, Jed Clampett and Barnaby Jones, Buddy Ebsen was a song-and-dance man who starred in such musicals as *Born to Dance* (1936), *Captain January* (1936) and *Broadway Melody of 1938* (1937). He was originally cast as the Tin Man in *The Wizard of Oz*, but Jack Haley took over the role when it was discovered that Ebsen had a life-threatening allergic reaction to the aluminum-based make-up.

Ebsen lived in this bay-front home on Balboa Island in Newport Beach during the 1970s and 1980s. The house looks out across Newport Bay to the Balboa Peninsula. Co-author Judy Artunian lived on Balboa Island during the same period and often saw Ebsen sitting in front of his house, greeting passersby who recognized him.

Buddy Ebsen
530 South Bay Front, Balboa Island

Nelson Eddy (1901–1967)
166 Ashdale Place, Brentwood

Nelson Eddy was an accomplished opera singer when Hollywood recruited him to sing in a handful of movies, including the *Dancing Lady* (1933) starring Joan Crawford and Clark Gable. Eddy was then teamed with singer Jeanette MacDonald for several operettas, starting with *Naughty Marietta* (1935). The duo amassed a huge following of "MacEddy" fans.

Eddy lived in this Brentwood house during the 1950s. He built a larger home in the same area many years earlier. When he first arrived in California in the early 1930s, Eddy shared a small house in Beverly Hills with his mother.

Sally Eilers (1908–1978)
3072 Motor Avenue, Cheviot Hills

In her first important role, Sally Eilers starred as a man-chasing fashion model in *Bad Girl* (1931). Eilers went on to land the plum role of a trapeze artist in the box office hit *State Fair* (1933), followed by several melodramas, including *They Made Her a Spy* (1939).

Eilers lived in the tranquil residential community of Cheviot Hills during the 1950s. In the 1920s, several movie studios cropped up in nearby Culver City, which today is the home of Sony Pictures.

Nelson Eddy
166 Ashdale Place, Brentwood

Douglas Fairbanks (1883–1939)
705 Palisades Beach Road, Santa Monica

One of Hollywood's first superstars, Douglas Fairbanks thrilled moviegoers with his athletic performances in such swashbucklers as *The Three Musketeers* (1921) and *Robin Hood* (1922). Fairbanks was also one of the four founders of United Artists and served as a screenwriter under the pseudonyms

"Elton Banks" and "Elton Thomas." Fairbanks' 16-year marriage to Mary Pickford was Hollywood's first block-buster romance.

When Fairbanks and Mary Pickford divorced, Pickfair went to Pickford in the divorce settlement, while Fairbanks kept this Santa Monica beach house. He and his new wife, Sylvia, settled here in 1939. Fairbanks died of a heart attack at the house in December of that year.

Douglas Fairbanks, Jr. (1909–2000)
1515 Amalfi Drive, Pacific Palisades

The son of silent star Douglas Fairbanks and his first wife, Beth, Doug, Jr., surprised some in Hollywood when he held his own opposite Edward G. Robinson in *Little Caesar* (1930), one of his first roles. He appeared in many more hits, including *The Prisoner of Zenda* (1937) and *Gunga Din* (1939).

Fairbanks and his second wife, Mary Lee Hartford, purchased this estate overlooking the Pacific coast in 1939. While Fairbanks served in World War II, Cary Grant and his then-wife, Woolworth heiress Barbara Hutton, rented the house. The house was later purchased by director Steven Spielberg.

Peter Falk (1927–)
1004 North Roxbury Drive, Beverly Hills

His gravely voice and glass eye give Peter Falk a distinctive quality in every part he plays. While his best-loved role may be his TV character, *Columbo*, Falk also turned in highly acclaimed performances in *Murder, Inc.* (1960), *Pocketful of Miracles* (1961), *Murder By Death* (1976) and the original version of *The In-Laws* (1979).

Peter Falk's Mediterranean-style house in Beverly Hills is one of the homes on a two-block stretch of North Roxbury where many celebrities lived, including composer Ira Gershwin, writer Dorothy Parker, and actors Lionel Barrymore, Lucille Ball and Marlene Dietrich.

Mia Farrow (1945–)
809 North Roxbury Drive, Beverly Hills

Mia Farrow was raised in a show-business household as the child of actress Maureen O'Sullivan and writer-director John Farrow. Her first major role was in the blockbuster thriller *Rosemary's Baby* (1968). She went on to star opposite Robert DeNiro in *The Great Gatsby* (1974), then teamed with Woody Allen for several critically acclaimed movies, including *Zelig* (1983), *Broadway Danny Rose* (1984) and *Hannah and Her Sisters* (1986).

Farrow grew up in this house. In her memoir, she wrote that this was the house "…where my family had lived and where my father had died." Ann Sothern later rented the house and let Farrow stay here for three weeks in 1963 while filming the pilot for the TV show *Peyton Place*.

W.C. Fields (1880–1946)
655 Funchal Road, Bel Air

W.C. Fields' stock character was a con artist who had a habit of making snide remarks under his breath. *It's a Gift* (1934), *You Can't Cheat an Honest Man* (1941) and *The Bank Dick* (1940), are among his best-loved movies. Fields wrote many of his own scripts under the names "Charles Bogle," "Mahatma Kane Jeeves" and "Otis Criblecoblis."

Fields lived here from the mid-1930s to the early 1940s. To avoid the responsibilities of homeownership, Fields rented all of his homes during his lifetime.

Mia Farrow
809 North Roxbury Drive, Beverly Hills

Carrie Fisher (1956–)
1700 Coldwater Canyon Drive, Los Angeles

Carrie Fisher earned legions of fans after appearing as Princess Lea in *Star Wars* (1977). Her screen debut was two years earlier when she played a flirtatious teenager in *Shampoo* (1975). The daughter of 1950's icons Debbie Reynolds and Eddie Fisher, Carrie Fisher co-starred in *Star Wars* sequels and

other box office hits, including *Hannah and Her Sisters* (1986) and *When Harry Met Sally* (1989). By the early 1990s, Fisher had turned to writing, producing several novels as well as the screenplay for *Postcards From the Edge* (1990).

Fisher bought the hacienda-style house behind these gates in 1993. When film costume designer Edith Head owned the property, the house was on five acres. Head eventually subdivided the property.

Errol Flynn (1909–1959)
8946 Appian Way, Hollywood Hills

Errol Flynn played light-hearted adventurers in such movies as *Captain Blood* (1935), *The Adventures of Robin Hood* (1938) and *The Dawn Patrol* (1938). Off screen, Flynn reinforced his daring-do image by living the life of Hollywood's reigning playboy of the 1930s and 1940s.

Flynn briefly lived in this Appian Way house while married to actress Lili Damita in the late 1930s. While they separated, he moved into a house he built that was also in the Hollywood Hills. The site of Flynn's many infamous parties, the Hollywood Hills house was later torn down.

Errol Flynn
8946 Appian Way, Hollywood Hills

Henry Fonda (1905–1982)
La Hacienda Apartments
149 South Roxbury Drive, Beverly Hills

To many film fans, Henry Fonda will always be the idealistic Tom Joad from *The Grapes of Wrath* (1940). Usually cast as likeable characters, Fonda exhibited an all-American charm in movies ranging from *The Lady Eve* (1941) to *Mister Roberts* (1955). Fonda won the Academy Award for Best Actor for his last film, *On Golden Pond* (1981). It was produced by his daughter, Jane Fonda.

Fonda hung his hat at this Beverly Hills apartment south of Wilshire in the mid-1930s. A few years later he shared a Brentwood house with actor James Stewart.

Joan Fontaine (1917–)
13030 Mulholland Drive, Los Angeles

Joan Fontaine was tapped by Alfred Hitchcock to star in two of his early classics. She played the young bride haunted by the ghost of Laurence Olivier's first wife in *Rebecca* (1940). In *Suspicion* (1941) she was again a bride, this time terrified that Cary Grant was plotting to kill her. Fontaine's performance in *Suspicion* earned her the Oscar for Best Actress. Her later movies include *The Affairs of Susan* (1945) and *Voyage to the Bottom of the Sea* (1961). Fontaine and her sister, actress Olivia de Havilland, have carried on a public rivalry for years.

Fontaine lived in a secluded house on this Mulholland-area property during the 1950s. Earlier in her career she lived in Beverly Hills.

Henry Fonda
La Hacienda Apartments, 149 South Roxbury Drive, Beverly Hills

Glenn Ford (1916–)
911 Oxford Way, Beverly Hills

Glenn Ford made more than 100 movies in his 54-year career. He became an established star after he appeared in *Gilda* (1946), opposite Rita Hayworth. Ford later earned kudos for his work in such films as *The Blackboard Jungle* (1955) and *The Rounders* (1965).

Shortly after divorcing dancer Eleanor Powell in 1959, Ford built this house on Oxford Way. He lived here as recently as 2000.

Harrison Ford (1942–)
1420 Braeridge Drive, Los Angeles

Harrison Ford's breakout role was that of the young spaceship captain, Han Solo, in *Star Wars* (1977). As he aged, Harrison took on the modern version of Hollywood's rugged leading-man roles. These include adventurer Dr. Henry "Indiana" Jones in *Raiders of the Lost Ark* (1981) and its sequels; the sensitive cop, John Book, in *Witness* (1985) and the diabolical Dr. Richard Kimball in *The Fugitive* (1993).

This charcoal-colored house trimmed in white is at the end of a short, quiet street. Ford lived here in the mid-1980s. He worked as a carpenter while trying to break into movies. In 1987, when he decided to add guest quarters and a barn to his property along the Snake River in Wyoming, Ford prepared detailed plans and helped with the construction.

Harrison Ford
1420 Braeridge Drive, Los Angeles

Annette Funicello (1942–)
16102 Sandy Lane, Encino

The star quality that Annette Funicello exhibited on *The Mickey Mouse Club* TV series (1955–1959) prompted The Walt Disney Company to sign her to recording and movie contracts when the series ended. As a teenager she starred in such movies as *Beach Party* (1963) and *Beach Blanket Bingo* (1965).

Funicello is among the many Hollywood personalities who have settled in Encino since the 1930s. This single-level house sits among many like it in a quiet residential neighborhood. Funicello has owned it since the late 1980s.

Clark Gable (1901–1960)
1609 North Normandie Avenue, Los Feliz
4543 Tara Drive, Encino

Although a studio boss once dismissed a young Clark Gable for looking like a gorilla, Gable's screen presence proved to be irresistible to moviegoers. So strong was the public clamor for him to play Rhett Butler in *Gone With the Wind* (1939), that Gable acquiesced to his fan's wishes even though he felt uncomfortable in period costumes. Gable earned the Best Actor Oscar for his performance in the romantic comedy, *It Happened One Night* (1934).

1609 North Normandie Avenue: Gable lived in this modest brick apartment building the year before he landed his breakout role in *Red Dust* (1932).

4543 Tara Drive: In the late 1930s, Gable and his third wife, actress Carole Lombard, bought this 27-acre ranch in Encino, which had previously belonged to director Raoul Walsh. Gable and Lombard filled their house with early American-style furnishings. What was once the ranch is today an upscale housing tract that includes the residence behind this gate. It was Gable and Lombard's original ranch house.

Greta Garbo (1905–1990)
1027 Chevy Chase Drive, Beverly Hills

In 1924, MGM brought Greta Garbo from Sweden to Hollywood as a favor to director Mauritz Stiller. It turned out to be a winning gamble for the studio. Garbo was a hit as the temptress in *Flesh and the Devil* (1926). It was the first of several silent movies in which she starred opposite John Gilbert, who was also her off-screen lover. Although critics sometimes pan Garbo's acting in talking pictures as being overly dramatic, she continued to draw audiences to her later hits, including *Grand Hotel* (1932), *Camille* (1937) and *Ninotchka* (1939).

In 1929, Garbo rented this three-bedroom Beverly Hills house. It was considered modest by Hollywood standards. When Garbo first arrived in California, she lived at the Miramar Hotel in Santa Monica.

Ava Gardner (1922–1990)
1637 North Vine Street, Hollywood

Ava Gardner's performance in *The Killers* (1942) put her on the Hollywood map. Gardner later won significant parts in *Show Boat* (1951), *Mogambo* (1953) and *On the Beach* (1959). Off-screen, Gardner's stormy marriages to Mickey Rooney, Artie Shaw and Frank Sinatra provided constant fodder for fan magazines.

MGM arranged for Gardner to stay here, at what was once the Hollywood Plaza Hotel, when she arrived in Hollywood in 1941. Bette Davis and many other stars lived at Hollywood Plaza early in their careers. Clara Bow's "It Café" was located in the hotel during the 1920s. The Motion Picture Hall of Fame is scheduled to open in this building in January 2005.

Judy Garland (1922–1969)
2605 Ivanhoe Drive, Silver Lake
8850 Evanview Drive, Hollywood Hills

During an era when Hollywood cultivated actresses who could also sing and dance, Judy Garland may have been the best of the bunch. As a teenager she played the indomitable Dorothy in *The Wizard of Oz* (1939), and staged elaborate neighborhood shows with Mickey Rooney in the *Andy Hardy* series (1938–1943). Critics also praised Garland's performances in such movies as *Meet Me in St. Louis* (1944), *Easter Parade* (1948) and *A Star is Born* (1954).

2605 Ivanhoe Drive: As a youngster, Garland lived with her parents and sisters in two successive hillside houses in Los Angeles' Silver Lake neighborhood. Although the family was struggling financially, Garland's father insisted that they live in grand style. There was a gym underneath the living room of this house.

8850 Evanview Drive: After Garland married director Vincent Minnelli in 1945, the couple moved into Minnelli's Evanview house. They bought vacant lots on either side of the house so that they could add a nursery for baby Liza, and a large bathroom and dressing room for Judy.

James Garner (1928–)
11492 Thurston Circle, Brentwood

For James Garner, TV seemed to be the ticket to movie stardom. After his TV series *Maverick* (1957–60) was over, important movie roles came his way. He appeared in some of the most admired movies of the 1960s, including *The Great Escape* (1963), *The Americanization of Emily* (1964) and *Grand Prix* (1966). Garner returned to TV to star in *The Rockford Files* (1974–80), then resumed his big-screen career with such movies as *Victor/Victoria* (1982) and *Murphy's Romance* (1985).

In the early 1960s, Garner and his family lived in this 2,950-square-foot house in Brentwood. It afforded the family more space than the three-bedroom apartment they shared while Garner starred in *Maverick*.

Greer Garson (1903–1996)
680 North Stone Canyon Road, Bel Air

Greer Garson was working at a London advertising agency when she began auditioning for roles in local theatre productions. A decade later she landed her first movie role, playing Mrs. Chips in *Goodbye Mr. Chips* (1939). Garson's performance earned her a nomination for the Best Actress Oscar. Three years later she won the honor for her work in *Mrs. Miniver* (1942). Garson's other hits included *Mrs. Parkington* (1944) and *The Valley of Decision* (1945), playing opposite Gregory Peck in one of his first major roles.

This 12-room, Tudor-style mansion was home to Garson during some of the busiest years of her career. Her estate included a 50-foot swimming pool. Garson, an accomplished pianist, kept two grand pianos in her living room.

Janet Gaynor (1906–1984)
2074 Watsonia Terrace, Whitley Heights

Janet Gaynor became a formidable star during the first two decades of her career. Gaynor earned the Oscar for Best Actress at the first Academy Awards ceremony for her performance as a Parisian street urchin in *Seventh Heaven* (1927). She also starred in *Sunrise* (1927), *The Farmer Takes a Wife* (1935) and the original *A Star Is Born* (1937).

Gaynor and her husband, the costume designer known simply as Adrian, lived here during the 1940s. Gloria Swanson stayed here while filming *Sunset Boulevard*, and in the 1930s, writer William Faulkner rented a studio that was attached to the house. The house, known as Villa Vallombrosa, is now a Los Angeles Historic-Cultural Monument.

Janet Gaynor
2074 Watsonia Terrace, Whitley Heights

Mitzi Gaynor (1931–)
610 North Arden Drive, Beverly Hills

Mitzi Gaynor's starring role as Nellie Forbush in the splashy musical *South Pacific* (1958) was the high-light of her 13-year movie career. Gaynor also starred with Bing Crosby in *Anything Goes* (1956) and with Gene Kelly in *Les Girls* (1957).

Gaynor and her husband, producer and agent Jack Bean, have lived here since 1960. The wooden fireplace in the living room is painted to resemble black marble. Gaynor told the *Los Angeles Times* that she learned from playwright Noel Coward that "If you have a fireplace, you're never lonesome." Most of the artifacts from her career are in storage. "I don't want my home to be a shrine to myself," she said.

Ben Gazzara (1930–)
661 Woodruff Avenue, Westwood

Ben Gazzara left a sizzling New York stage career in 1957 when he came to Hollywood to make a drama called *The Strange One* (1957). Gazzara quickly became known for fueling his characters with intensity in such movies as *Anatomy of a Murder* (1959), *Husbands* (1970) and *The Spanish Prisoner* (1998).

Gazzara's residence during the 1960s is a Neo-Classic design dominated by a row of two-story columns. It's located a few blocks from the UCLA campus.

John Gilbert (1899–1936)
Los Angeles Athletic Club
131 West Seventh Street, Los Angeles

John Gilbert was one of the silent screen's hottest matinee idols. His signature films include *The Big Parade* (1925) and three pairings with Greta Garbo: *Flesh and the Devil* (1926), *Love* (1927) and *Queen Christina* (1933).

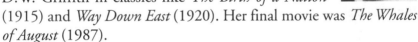

As a fledgling actor in 1916, Gilbert lived at the Hotel Santa Monica. By 1921 Gilbert had moved to the upscale Los Angeles Athletic Club. In 1924, he built a Spanish Colonial house (since demolished) near Beverly Hills.

Lillian Gish (1983–1993)
610 South Serrano Avenue, Los Angeles

Lillian Gish was a delicate beauty who became one of Hollywood's first A-list actors. She got her start with D.W. Griffith in classics like *The Birth of a Nation* (1915) and *Way Down East* (1920). Her final movie was *The Whales of August* (1987).

While living here in the late teens Gish wrote to a friend, "I still like apartments best. Have only been home to sleep since we have had it [the house] as we work night and day, worked Xmas eve until ten thirty, was made up ready to work at eight o'clock Xmas morning did not finish till 9:30 that evening, the same on New Year's and Sunday, so you see it doesn't matter much where I live." (This building's address was 616 when Gish lived here.)

Paulette Goddard (1911–1990)
1464 Lindacrest Drive, Los Angeles

It wasn't uncommon for Charlie Chaplin's supporting characters to live on as movie icons. That was the case for the bright-eyed waif that Paulette Goddard played in Charlie Chaplin's *Modern Times* (1936). Goddard, who became Chaplin's third wife in 1936, was also featured in Chaplin's *The Great Dictator* (1940). In between, she appeared in *The Women* (1939) and two Bob Hope movies: *The Cat and the Canary* (1939) and *The Ghost Breakers* (1940). She later earned an Oscar nomination for her portrayal of a sarcastic nurse in *So Proudly We Hail!* (1943).

Goddard bought this Normandy-style house in 1942. A decade later she divorced her third husband, actor Burgess Meredith, then sold the house and moved to New York.

Cuba Gooding, Jr. (1968–)
3200 Coldwater Canyon Avenue, Studio City

In his still-young career, Cuba Gooding, Jr., may be best known for his Oscar-winning performance as the exuberant football player in *Jerry McGuire* (1996) who badgers Tom Cruise with the taunt, "Show me the money!" Gooding

was also praised for his performance opposite Jack Nicholson in *As Good As It Gets* (1997).

Gooding lived here in the mid-1990s when his career was starting to heat up. He later moved to a Pacific Palisades home where he installed a roller-hockey court.

Paulette Goddard
1464 Lindacrest Drive, Los Angeles

Leo Gorcey (1917–1969)
906-908 North Ogden Drive, West Hollywood

Leo Gorcey was the wise-guy leader of The Dead End Kids, Hollywood's version of a teenage gang circa 1938. The six Dead End Kids actors had starred in the Broadway play, *Dead End*, before heading to Hollywood to re-create their roles in a milder version of the play. After *The Dead End Kids* movies (1937–1939), Gorcey went on to appear in *East Side Kids* and *Bowery Boys* films.

This was Gorcey's home base during his Dead End Kids days. He once owned a home where he personally dug a hole and installed an 18-square-foot swimming pool. He later bought a ranch in Los Molinos in Northern California.

Louis Gossett, Jr. (1936–)
6614 Dume Drive, Malibu

Louis Gossett, Jr., bypassed a chance to play basketball for the New York Knicks in 1958 to nurture his acting career. For his first movie, Gossett repeated his Broadway role in *A Raisin in the Sun* (1961). Two decades later he earned the Academy Award for Best Supporting Actor for playing Richard Gere's drill sergeant in *An Officer and a Gentleman* (1982). Since the mid-1970s, Gossett has divided his time among movies, stage and TV.

Gossett's house is in the seaside community of Point Dume, where celebrities such as Bob Dylan and Martin Sheen have had homes for many years.

Betty Grable (1916–1973)
The Palmerston
1917 Palmerston Place, Los Feliz

Betty Grable's sunny, down-to-earth screen personality and photogenic legs seemed to be tailor-made for World War II-era films. The famous photo of Grable in a white swimsuit, looking over her shoulder, reinforced her girl-next-door-meets-sexy-pin-up-girl image. Grable excelled in musicals and lighthearted fare such as *Moon Over Miami* (1941) and *Pin Up Girl* (1944).

Grable settled into this Los Feliz apartment complex in the early 1930s. When she and her mother first arrived in Los Angeles in 1929, they lived at the Ambassador Hotel (3400 Wilshire Boulevard — see John Barrymore).

Cary Grant (1904–1986)
9966 Beverly Grove Drive, Los Angeles

Cary Grant, the epitome of the urbane gentleman, was equally adept at comedies and dramas. Grant starred in such comedies as *Bringing Up Baby* (1938) and *His Girl Friday* (1940). Among his hit dramas were *Indiscreet* (1958) and *North By Northwest* (1959).

Grant, who lived just a stone's throw from Beverly Hills, enjoyed views of the city from the house beyond this gate. Grant, a notorious clotheshorse, had a walk-in dressing room that was lined with mirrors on all sides. He lived here for several decades from the 1940s onward. Over the years, Grant also lived in West Hollywood (1400-1414 North Havenhurst Drive—see Louise Brooks and Virginia Cherrill), Los Feliz (2177 West Live Oak Drive—see Randolph Scott) and Santa Monica (1038 Palisades Beach Road—see Norma Talmadge).

Sydney Greenstreet (1879–1954)
1531 Selma Drive, Hollywood Hills

Fans of *The Maltese Falcon* (1941) and *Casablanca* (1942) know the portly Sydney Greenstreet, if not by name, then by his villainous presence. *The Maltese Falcon* was Greenstreet's film debut. His performance as Humphrey

Bogart's nemesis with the evil laugh earned him an Academy Award nomination. Greenstreet continued to be in demand for comedic and dramatic roles until he retired in 1952.

This corner house, near the intersection of the Sunset Strip and Laurel Canyon, was Greenstreet's last home.

Virginia Grey (1917–)
4543 Densmore Avenue, Encino

Virginia Grey was a comely blonde who appeared in more than 100 movies from 1927 to 1970. She was 10 years old when she won her first role: Little Eva in *Uncle Tom's Cabin* (1927). Grey went on to play supporting parts and the occasional lead role. *Idiot's Delight* (1939), *The Big Store* (1941) and *Back Street* (1961) are among her more well-known films.

Grey lived in this Tudor-inspired house in Encino when she was making such movies as *The Restless Years* (1958) and *Tammy Tell Me True* (1961).

Corrine Griffith (1894–1979)
1030 Benedict Canyon Drive, Beverly Hills

Corrine Griffith entered the movies in 1917 after winning a Santa Monica beauty contest. Griffith's biggest box office success was the drama *The Divine Lady* (1928). She ran her own production unit at First National where she made *Lilies of the Field* (1924), a story she chose to re-tool for her first talking picture six years later. After retiring from the screen, Griffith wrote six books, including *Papa's Delicate Condition*, which became a 1963 movie.

Griffith bought the Tudor Revival house located up this curving driveway in 1924, shortly after it was built. Actor Ronald Colman made some modifications to the house when he bought it in 1935. Among Griffith's many real estate investments was a commercial area of Beverly Hills known as "Four Corners," located at the intersection of South Beverly Drive and Charleville.

Buddy Hackett (1924–2003)
800 North Whittier Drive, Beverly Hills

Buddy Hackett, the chubby comedian who sounded like his mouth was full of cotton, played likeable, silly characters in *The Music Man* (1962), *It's a Mad Mad Mad Mad World* (1963) and *The Love Bug* (1969). He also lent his voice to the seagull in the Disney film *The Little Mermaid* (1989).

A life-like statue of an elephant stands amid the plants in front of this house where Hackett lived during the last several decades of his life. The elephant also stood guard at Hackett's previous Beverly Hills house.

William "Billy" Haines (1900–1973)
1712 North Stanley Avenue, Hollywood Hills

William "Billy" Haines was a top box office draw during the silent era, often playing the smart aleck "big man on campus" in such movies as *Brown of Harvard* (1926) and *West Point* (1927). He also appeared opposite Marion Davies in *Show People* (1928). In the mid-1930s, Haines switched from acting to interior decorating. He ultimately earned more lasting fame in that field, designing home décor for the likes of Joan Crawford and the U.S. Ambassador to Great Britain.

In the mid-1920s, Haines bought this house located just north of West Hollywood. He turned it into the combination colonial New

Orleans and eighteenth century English-style home that stands today. MGM production head Irving Thalberg was so impressed with the interior design the first time he toured Haines' home, it's reported that he kept asking, "Who did this?" Haines replied simply, "I did."

Buddy Hackett
800 North Whittier Drive, Beverly Hills

Alan Hale (1892–1950)
1940 Outpost Circle, Hollywood Hills

Burly Alan Hale was a versatile character actor who appeared in nearly 200 movies, ranging from the Rudolph Valentino drama, *The Four Horsemen of the*

Apocalypse (1921) to the early screwball comedy *It Happened One Night* (1934). Hale also directed several movies for Cecil B. DeMille in the 1920s. His son, Alan Hale Jr., starred as The Skipper on TV's *Gilligan's Island.*

Hale bought this home in Outpost Estates in 1935. The five-bedroom Mediterranean-style house featured a grand rotunda area. The house stayed in the Hale family for several decades.

Jack Haley (1898–1979)
600 Walden Drive, Beverly Hills

Jack Haley was featured in several musicals, including Shirley Temple's *Poor Little Rich Girl* (1936), before he landed the role of his life—the Tin Man in *The Wizard of Oz* (1939). Haley's light touch with dialogue and music was featured in several more musicals and comedies before he

went into semi-retirement at approximately age 50.

During their *Wizard of Oz* days, Haley lived within a mile or so of the Cowardly Lion's (Bert Lahr) house at 604 North Palm Drive, and the Scarecrow's (Ray Bolger) house at 618 North Beverly Drive.

George Hamilton (1939–)
1100 Carolyn Way, Beverly Hills

Famous for his perpetual suntan and smile, George Hamilton's early career was dominated by dramas, including *Where the Boys Are* (1960) and *Two Weeks in Another Town* (1962). Hamilton gained more acclaim when he switched to such comedies as *Love at First Bite* (1979).

Hamilton at one time owned this historic, 30-room Grayhall mansion. The house was built in 1916 by a Boston banker and was substantially upgraded in 1920 by Silsby Spalding, who later became the first mayor of Beverly Hills. Douglas Fairbanks rented Grayhall while Pickfair was under construction.

Margaret Hamilton (1902–1985)
1807 Courtney Avenue, Hollywood Hills

She is so closely identified with her *Wizard of Oz* (1939) characters that many fans swear that Margaret Hamilton was born to play the shrewish Miss Gulch and the terrifying Wicked Witch of the West. Hamilton was a kindergarten and nursery school teacher before she turned to acting. She became an expert at portraying carping, disapproving women in such movies as *A Slight Case of Murder* (1938) and *My Little Chickadee* (1940).

In the mid-1930s, Hamilton lived with her husband and young son in this elegant apartment, a quick broom ride from Hollywood Boulevard. Hamilton later occupied two Beverly Hills houses, which have since been torn down. She relocated to New York City in 1950.

Tom Hanks (1956–)
956 Corsica Drive, Pacific Palisades

Tom Hanks, a modern Hollywood "everyman," first hooked movie audiences when he starred in *Splash* (1984). He went on to be featured in a string of comedies, including the critically acclaimed *Big* (1988). By the mid-1990s, Hanks was taking on more complex characters in such movies as *Philadelphia* (1993), as well as *Apollo 13* (1995) and *Saving Private Ryan* (1998)—two films that capitalize on his fascination with space travel and World War II, respectively. Hanks earned back-to-back Best Actor Oscars for *Philadelphia* and *Forest Gump* (1994).

Hanks bought this house in the 1990s. He and his family have since moved to a more private Pacific Palisades home. In 2002, they completed construction on a five-house estate in Sun Valley, Idaho.

Tom Hanks
956 Corsica Drive, Pacific Palisades

Oliver Hardy (1892–1957)
4425 Russell Avenue, Los Feliz
621 Alta Drive, Beverly Hills

Oliver Hardy was the rotund, fastidious and perpetually exasperated member of the Laurel & Hardy comedy team. Although Hardy and Stan Laurel shared the screen in several movies, they didn't become an official team until producer Hal Roach paired them together in the 1927 comedy short, *Putting Pants on Phillip.* Unlike many of their peers, Laurel & Hardy easily made the switch from silents to talkies, reworking—and in some cases improving upon—many of their silent hits. Before turning to acting in 1914, Hardy was a singer and a movie theater manager.

4425 Russell Avenue: Hardy lived in this Los Feliz house during the 1920s. He kept this house for many years after taking up residence in Beverly Hills.

621 Alta Drive: By the early 1930s, Hardy had settled into this larger house in Beverly Hills. In the 1940s, Hardy and his third wife, Lucille, moved to a ranch in Van Nuys.

Oliver Hardy
621 Alta Drive, Beverly Hills

Jean Harlow (1911–1937)
1353 Club View Drive, Los Angeles

She wasn't the screen's first platinum blonde, but Jean Harlow was the epitome of the blonde bombshell of the 1930s. One of her first major roles was in a movie called, appropriately enough, *Platinum Blonde* (1931). The following year Harlow made *Red Dust* (1932), which featured several incendiary scenes with Clark Gable. At the age of 26, Harlow died suddenly of uremic poisoning while filming *Saratoga* (1937).

Shortly after making her first movie, Harlow purchased this home just outside of Beverly Hills. She later relocated with her mother and stepfather to a larger Holmby Hills estate.

Richard Harris (1930–2002)
600 Saint Cloud Road, Bel Air

American audiences embraced Irishman Richard Harris after seeing him play King Arthur in the hit musical *Camelot* (1967). He followed that with a variety of roles in adventures and dramas, including *A Man Called Horse* (1970), and two films that were awarded the Best Picture Oscar, *Unforgiven* (1992) and *Gladiator* (2000).

Although Harris preferred living abroad, he stayed in Southern California when his shooting schedule called for it. Harris resided in the Bel Air house behind these vine-covered gates around the time *Camelot* was released.

Jean Harlow
1353 Club View Drive, Los Angeles

Rex Harrison (1908–1990)
9554 Hidden Valley Road, Los Angeles

After distinguishing himself in *The Citadel* (1938) and other British movies, Rex Harrison was lured to Hollywood with movie offers in 1946. The debonair Harrison starred in some of the most popular American movies, including *The Ghost and Mrs. Muir* (1947), *Unfaithfully Yours* (1948) and *My Fair Lady* (1964).

Harrison lived in this Hidden Valley house while making *My Fair Lady*. In the 1950s, Harrison lived in the San Fernando Valley to be close to Warner Brothers Studios.

William S. Hart (1866–1946)
8341 De Longpre Avenue, West Hollywood

William S. Hart was 45 when he made his debut in a movie called *His Hour of Manhood* (1914). Within a few years he became a popular screen cowboy. Throughout the silent era, Hart co-wrote, produced and directed many of his films. By the time he retired in the mid-1920s, Hart had amassed a small fortune. He went on to purchase real estate throughout the Los Angeles area.

Hart's West Hollywood house, where he lived in the 1920s, is now part of William S. Hart Memorial Park. After retiring from films in 1925, he built the Horseshoe Ranch in Newhall (located in the northern part of Los Angeles County), and lived there until his death two decades later. Hart deeded the land to the county, stipulating it be "dedicated to the people of every race and creed."

William S. Hart
8341 De Longpre Avenue, West Hollywood

Goldie Hawn (1945–)
788 Amalfi Drive, Pacific Palisades

The seemingly ageless Goldie Hawn grabbed the studios' attention with her role as a ditsy girl on the popular TV show, *Rowan and Martin's Laugh-In* (1968–1970). Hawn went on to star in, and sometimes produce, such light comedies as *Private Benjamin* (1980), *House Sitter* (1992) and *First Wives Club* (1996). Hawn's daughter is actress Kate Hudson.

Hawn and actor Kurt Russell lived in this Pacific Palisades house from the mid-1980s until the early 1990s. In the late 1960s, while shooting the TV show *Laugh-In*, Hawn lived in a New England-style house in Bel Air with her first husband, Gus. At the time she told a reporter that she loved to clean house.

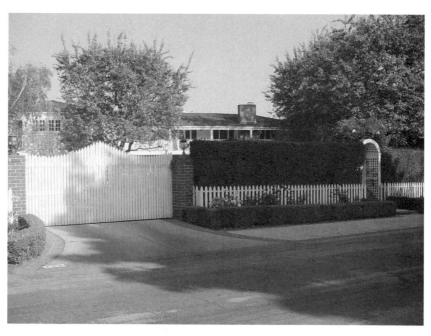

Susan Hayward (1918–1975)
3801 Longridge Avenue, Sherman Oaks

Susan Hayward won an Academy Award for Best Actress for her portrayal of a woman who, though falsely accused of murder, is on her way to the gas chamber in *I Want To Live!* (1958). Earlier, Hayward earned praise for playing women who prevail over disaster in such movies as *Smash Up—The Story of a Woman* (1947), *With a Song in My Heart* (1952) and *I'll Cry Tomorrow* (1955).

Hayward moved into this San Fernando Valley estate in the late 1940s. While house hunting, Hayward and her family stayed at the Miramar Hotel in Santa Monica. During her house hunt she complained that too many home sellers expected buyers to purchase the furniture—at inflated prices—along with the house.

Van Heflin (1910–1971)
116 North Tigertail Road, Brentwood

Van Heflin appeared in films and on Broadway for more than 10 years before movie fans really took notice of him. He earned the Academy Award for Best Supporting Actor for 1942's *Johnny Eager*. Heflin was also memorable as the homesteader who wins Alan Ladd's support in *Shane* (1953).

After he divorced his wife of 25 years, Heflin moved out of this Brentwood mansion and into a Hollywood-area apartment. A few years later he suffered a fatal heart attack while swimming in the apartment complex pool.

Paul Henreid (1908–1992)
255 Chadbourne Avenue, Brentwood

Paul Henried is best remembered for two movies released back-to-back. In *Now Voyager* (1942) he played Bette Davis's debonair paramour whose trademark was lighting two cigarettes and handing one to her. In *Casablanca* (1942) he was Victor Laszlo, the Czech freedom fighter who flies off with Ingrid Bergman at the end of the movie.

Shortly before the Hungarian-born Henreid and his wife, Elizabeth, moved to this Brentwood estate, they hosted a dinner party at their Westwood apartment. In his memoir, Henreid recalled that only one

person showed up. The Henreids, who had been in the United States for less than a year, hadn't realized that their party was on Thanksgiving Day.

Audrey Hepburn (1929–1993)
100 Delfern Drive, Holmby Hills

The elegant, intriguing Audrey Hepburn won her first Academy Award for Best Actress for her portrayal of a princess who escapes her royal duties with the help of a reporter, played by Gregory Peck, in *Roman Holiday* (1953). Her next Oscar was for the role that seemed to have been written for her: Holly Golightly in *Breakfast at Tiffany's* (1961). Hepburn also starred as Eliza Doolittle in the blockbuster musical *My Fair Lady* (1964).

Hepburn considered her house in Switzerland to be her full-time home. While filming *My Fair Lady*, she and her husband, Mel Ferrer, rented this eclectic, Neo-classic-style mansion on the corner of Delfern and Sunset.

Katharine Hepburn (1907–2003)
1050 Summit Drive, Beverly Hills

Katharine Hepburn's reign as one of Hollywood's most respected actresses began with her portrayal of an eager young actress in *Morning Glory* (1933). That performance earned Hepburn the first of four Academy Awards for Best Actress. Hepburn's other Oscars were for *The Philadelphia Story* (1940), *The Lion in Winter* (1968) and *On Golden Pond* (1981). She also played memorable characters in *Adam's Rib* (1949), *The African Queen* (1951) and many other classics.

By the 1940s, Hepburn was spending much of her time between films in Connecticut. Beginning in 1947, Hepburn lived at this Beverly Hills home of Irene Selznick (ex-wife of producer David O. Selznick) when she worked in Hollywood. Hepburn made the home her own, decorating it with African artifacts she had collected while shooting *The African Queen* on location.

Charlton Heston (1924–)
2859 Coldwater Canyon Drive, Los Angeles

Charlton Heston first displayed his commanding screen presence when he played a hard-bitten circus manager in *The Greatest Show on Earth* (1952). Heston went on to play bigger-than-life characters in such movies as *The Ten Commandments* (1956), *Ben-Hur* (1959), *El Cid* (1961) and *The Agony and The Ecstasy* (1965). Away from the screen, Heston was the president of the Screen Actors Guild from 1965–1971.

Heston built a house on this property in the late 1950s. Impressed by the wide expanse of open land and the panoramic views, Heston bought the lot on the first day he saw it. His father supervised the home's construction.

William Holden (1918–1981)
Hollywood Athletic Club
6525 West Sunset Boulevard, Hollywood

William Holden's portrayal of a young boxer in *Golden Boy* (1939) launched a storied career that lasted 43 years. Holden, known for his unaffected acting style, turned in much-lauded performances in *Sunset Boulevard* (1950), *Stalag 17* (1953), *The Bridge on the River Kwai* (1957) and *Network* (1976).

Holden lived at the Hollywood Athletic Club in the late 1930s. He later moved to a house in North Hollywood that was purchased by actor Denzel Washington in 1987 (4701 Sancola Avenue—see Denzel Washington).

Bob Hope (1903–2003)
4217 Navajo Street, Toluca Lake
10346 Moorpark Street, Toluca Lake

Bob Hope appeared in dozens of comedies from the 1930s to the late 1970s, but his most popular movies were the "Road" pictures he did with Bing Crosby and Dorothy Lamour. Hope's show business activities extended well beyond movies. He reeled off his trademark one-liners on his radio and TV programs and in the shows he presented to U.S. troops overseas.

4217 Navajo Street: In 1938, Hope leased this Streamline-Modern style house from animator Walter Lantz. He held script meetings in the evenings here for his new radio program, "The Bob Hope Pepsodent Show." During that same year, Hope also made his film debut in *The Big Broadcast of 1938.*

10346 Moorpark Street: Hope and his wife, Dorothy, paid $28,000 for this Toluca Lake house in 1940. When they moved in it had a leaky roof. They not only fixed the roof, they upgraded the entire house and eventually bought the surrounding property to create a nine-acre estate.

Bo Hopkins (1942–)
6628 Ethel Avenue, North Hollywood

Best known for playing off-kilter characters in such movies as *The Wild Bunch* (1969) and *The Getaway* (1972), Bo Hopkins has been featured in scores of Westerns and action movies since making his screen debut in 1969. Hopkins has also appeared in *The Day of the Locust* (1975) and *The Newton Boys* (1998).

During *The Wild Bunch* years, Hopkins lived in this house in North Hollywood, a suburb once described by historian David Gebhard as "the poor northern sister of the Hollywood over the hill."

Leslie Howard (1893–1943)
606 North Camden Drive, Beverly Hills

The mild-mannered Ashley Wilkes in *Gone With the Wind* (1939) wasn't Leslie Howard's favorite role, but it proved to be his most enduring. Before that watershed role, Howard appeared in several Norma Shearer dramas, including the huge hit *Smilin' Through* (1932). He also worked opposite Bette Davis in *Of Human Bondage* (1934) and *The Petrified Forest* (1936), and later co-starred with Ingrid Bergman in *Intermezzo* (1939). Howard was a civilian casualty of World War II when an airplane he was riding in was shot down over Europe.

In 1939, the year *Gone With the Wind* was released, Howard and his family moved into this Beverly Hills house that had previously been owned by actress Hedy Lamarr.

Kim Hunter (1922–2002)
Sunset Marquis Hotel and Villas
1200 North Alta Loma Road, West Hollywood

Kim Hunter earned cult status by co-starring as an ape-like scientist in three *Planet of the Apes* movies (1968, 1970, 1971). Two decades earlier, Hunter won an Academy Award for Best Supporting Actress for a role she originated on Broadway: Stella

Kowalski in *A Streetcar Named Desire* (1951). Hunter was blacklisted for a time during the 1950s for her support of civil rights causes.

Hunter's home was New York, but she stayed in the Los Angeles area for extended periods while filming movies. In the early 1960s, Hunter—who was an accomplished cook— moved into an apartment in the Sunset Marquis Hotel and Villas, in part because it had a decent-sized kitchen.

Tab Hunter (1931–)
9080 Shoreham Drive, West Hollywood

One of the prototypical heartthrobs of the early 1960s, Tab Hunter began earning substantial roles after playing a naive soldier in the box office hit *Battle Cry* (1955). He went on to co-star in such movies as *That Kind of Woman* (1959) opposite Sophia Loren and *The Pleasure of His Company*

(1961) opposite Debbie Reynolds.

Hunter kept an apartment here during the 1950s. In 1988 he left Hollywood for Santa Fe, New Mexico. Today he lives in Santa Barbara.

Samuel L. Jackson (1948–)
5128 Encino Avenue, Encino

Samuel L. Jackson's career began to take shape when he joined New York's Negro Ensemble Company in 1976. While in New York he met Spike Lee and landed roles in three of Lee's movies: *Do the Right Thing* (1989), *Mo' Better Blues* (1990) and *Jungle Fever* (1991). Jackson's role in *Pulp Fiction* (1994) as a philosophy-spouting hit man earned him an Academy Award nomination in 1994.

Jackson bought this Tudor-style San Fernando Valley home in 1994. A guesthouse on the property served as Jackson's office and screening room.

Van Johnson (1916–)
801 North Foothill Road, Beverly Hills

Van Johnson played many a clean-cut young man in light comedies, often co-starring with the equally squeaky-clean June Allyson (they appeared in five movies together). Johnson was also cast in hit war movies like *Thirty Seconds Over Tokyo* (1944) and *Command Decision* (1948).

In 1949, Johnson and his wife moved from Santa Monica to this Beverly Hills house to be closer to their friends. Their new house was considerably smaller than the expansive Pacific Palisades mansion he had purchased several years earlier (757 Kingman Avenue, Pacific Palisades— see Dolores Del Rio).

Al Jolson (1886–1950)
4875 Louise Avenue, Encino

"Wait a minute, wait a minute. You ain't heard nothin' yet!" With those prophetic words spoken by Al Jolson in *The Jazz Singer* (1927), the talkies were officially born. That historic feature—in which Jolson played a young man who chose the life of a jazz singer against his parents' wishes—was his first movie. Jolson continued to portray singers, often performing in blackface.

Jolson was among the first group of Hollywood stars to view the San Fernando Valley as a sanctuary from the pressures of movie life. In 1935, he built a house on this property for his family. Like many Valley estates at the time, Jolson's included a fruit orchard.

Shirley Jones (1934–)
701 North Oakhurst Drive, Beverly Hills

An audition with composer Richard Rogers paved the way to Broadway and Hollywood for Shirley Jones. Rogers cast her in the lead role for the film versions of two of his hit musicals, *Oklahoma* (1955) and *Carousel* (1956). Although musicals were her forté, Jones earned the Academy Award for Best Supporting Actress for her performance as a bitter prostitute in *Elmer Gantry* (1960). Jones won new fans in the 1970s when she starred on TV as the matriarch on *The Partridge Family* (1970–74).

Jones bought this Beverly Hills house in 1965. Shortly before putting the house on the market in 2001, she and her husband, Marty Ingles, completed a $1.5 million remodeling project. Among their additions were a guesthouse and a video arcade room.

Boris Karloff (1887–1969)
714 North Foothill Road, Beverly Hills

Boris Karloff played plenty of heavies in silent films, but it wasn't until he starred as the silent monster in the 1931 talkie, *Frankenstein*, that he became one of Hollywood's favorite scary characters. Karloff also appeared in *The Mummy* (1932), *The Mask of Fu Manchu* (1932) and *The Son of Frankenstein* (1939).

Karloff lived a very un-Frankenstein life at home. He was an avid reader with a house full of books. He also loved tending to his garden and his many pets. This white house, with its stone walkway and chimney, was Karloff's home after he divorced his second wife in 1946.

Danny Kaye (1913–1987)
1103 San Ysidro Drive, Beverly Hills

Singing absurd lyrics and dashing through his scenes in a frenzy, the multi-talented Danny Kaye's first screen appearance was in *Up In Arms* (1944). Kaye's creative comedy can also be seen in such movies as *The Secret Life of Walter Mitty* (1947), *The Inspector General* (1949) and *The Court Jester* (1956), which featured his classic "The Chalice from the Palace" routine.

Danny Kaye and his wife, composer Sylvia Fine, bought this Beverly Hills estate in the mid-1940s. Two decades later, Kaye, a serious

cook, added a kitchen that was specially outfitted to prepare Chinese food. He hired workmen from the CBS Studios in Los Angeles to build the kitchen.

Boris Karloff
714 North Foothill Road, Beverly Hills

Buster Keaton (1895–1966)
855 Westchester Place, Los Angeles
1043 South Victoria Avenue, Los Angeles

Buster Keaton has been heralded as one of Hollywood's most innovative comic filmmakers. In almost every film he portrayed a young man dogged by bad luck, who nonetheless soldiers on to win the girl or save the day. His plots may have been simple but his acrobatic stunts could be complex and dangerous. From 1919 to 1928, Keaton wrote, directed and starred in such films as *Sherlock Jr.* (1924) and *The General* (1927), which are today considered ahead of their time. Just before the dawn of the talkies, Keaton lost his studio and rarely found roles that did justice to his talents. In 1960, The Academy of Motion Picture Arts and Sciences recognized his achievements by awarding him an honorary Oscar.

855 Westchester Place: Several years before he built his famous Italian Villa in Beverly Hills (1018 Pamela Drive — see James Mason), Keaton and his first wife, Natalie, bought their first house. At the time he told her he wanted a ranch in the San Fernando Valley. She insisted on a house in Los Angeles so they bought this one on Westchester in 1921. Keaton finally got his San Fernando Valley ranch decades later.

1043 South Victoria Avenue: In 1924, Keaton bought this bungalow for his mother and his younger brother and sister. During lean times after World War II, he wound up living here himself with his third wife, Eleanor.

Buster Keaton
1043 South Victoria Avenue, Los Angeles

Gene Kelly (1912–1996)
725 North Rodeo Drive, Beverly Hills

Gene Kelly's athletic dance performances stand out in nearly every movie in which he appears. Kelly tap-danced with cartoon characters in *Anchors Aweigh* (1945), matched the famed Nicholas Brothers step for step in *The Pirate* (1948), and took balletic turns to Gershwin music in *An American in Paris* (1951). Kelly may be best known for his rendition of the title song in *Singin' in the Rain* (1952), a musical which also included several memorable song-and-dance numbers with Donald O'Connor and Debbie Reynolds.

A fire destroyed Kelly's Rodeo Drive home in 1983, three days before Christmas. He reportedly lost everything he owned except for the pajamas he was wearing when he escaped the late-night fire. The next morning Kelly vowed to rebuild the house, and the following year, he did.

Grace Kelly (1929–1982)
1285 North Sweetzer Avenue, West Hollywood

The coolly elegant Grace Kelly got her big break when she was cast as Gary Cooper's wife in *High Noon* (1952). She went on to appear in *Mogambo* (1953), *Dial M for Murder* (1954), *Rear Window* (1954) and *To Catch a Thief* (1955). Kelly left her successful movie career behind when she married Prince Ranier III of Monaco in 1956.

Kelly shuttled back and forth between New York and Hollywood during the early 1950s, before settling into this West Hollywood apartment complex in 1954. The complex itself had been built a year earlier.

Gene Kelly
725 North Rodeo Drive, Beverly Hills

J. Warren Kerrigan (1879–1947)
1765 North Gower Street, Hollywood

In an era when movie audiences couldn't get enough Westerns, J. Warren "Jack" Kerrigan was among the top cowboy stars. He first appeared before the camera in 1910 and became a star after joining Universal in 1915. A few years later, he sabotaged his career by announcing that he would ignore his draft summons if called to serve in World War I. His career

briefly found new life after he was cast in the lead role in *The Covered Wagon* (1923).

Kerrigan lived in the heart of Hollywood in 1917, the same year he founded his own production company. A black fence protects this bright, white building.

Nicole Kidman (1967–)
1525 Sorrento Drive, Pacific Palisades

Nicole Kidman's acting career began with an Australian TV show in 1983. American moviegoers first took serious notice of Kidman when she played the cynical TV anchor in *To Die For* (1995). Kidman went on to win the Academy Award for Best Actress for playing writer Virginia Woolf in *The Hours* (2002).

From the early 1990s until their divorce in 2001, Kidman and her husband, Tom Cruise, lived on this Pacific Palisades estate. The house is only partially viewable from Sorrento. Walls wrap around the home's entire corner lot.

Percy Kilbride (1888–1964)
6650 Franklin Avenue, Hollywood

Percy Kilbride played the lethargic, suspender-clad Pa Kettle in the popular Ma and Pa Kettle movies, opposite Marjorie Main. The two first played the Kettle characters in *The Egg and I* (1947) starring Claudette Colbert and Fred MacMurray. Universal then starred Kilbride and Main in seven films starting with *Ma and Pa Kettle* (1949) and ending with *Ma and Pa Kettle in Waikiki* (1955).

In December of 1964, Kilbride was taking a stroll near his Franklin Avenue home when he was hit by a car. He died eight days later.

Alan Ladd (1913–1964)
323 North Mapleton Drive, Holmby Hills

For nearly a decade, Alan Ladd played minor roles, including an unaccredited appearance as a reporter in *Citizen Kane* (1941). He eventually graduated to starring roles, achieving movie immortality thanks to his performance as the heroic title character in the Western classic *Shane* (1953).

Ladd was very involved in designing the H-shaped Holmby Hills house behind these gates. The house was built in 1949. The Ladds decorated their home with country French-style furnishings.

Diane Ladd (1932–)
2241 Betty Lane, Los Angeles

Diane Ladd played Flo, the outspoken waitress who befriends Ellen Burstyn in *Alice Doesn't Live Here Anymore* (1974). She has played many Southern women throughout her career, including real-life daughter Laura Dern's mother in *Rambling Rose* (1991). Both women were nominated for an Academy Award for the film, marking the first time that a mother and daughter were nominated in the same year.

In the mid-1990s, Diane Ladd owned this corner house on Betty Lane, a short street off of Coldwater Canyon Drive that climbs steeply toward a tree-covered hillside.

Bert Lahr (1895–1967)
604 North Palm Drive, Beverly Hills

Bert Lahr is best remembered for his touching portrayal of the Cowardly Lion in *The Wizard of Oz* (1939). Lahr would later remark that the role ultimately limited his success in Hollywood because the studios insisted on typecasting him. He had better luck on Broadway where he earned a Tony Award in 1964.

Lahr left the New York stage in 1938 to follow his future wife to California. This house was the Lahr family's home in the early 1940s. In 1943, depressed over not getting a movie part he expected, he impulsively uprooted his family from Beverly Hills and moved back to New York.

Veronica Lake (1919–1973)
1559 North Beverly Drive, Los Angeles

Known primarily for the blond locks that swept over one eye, Veronica Lake co-starred with William Holden and Ray Milland in *I Wanted Wings* (1941), then was cast opposite Joel McCrea in *Sullivan's Travels* (1941). Lake was paired with Alan Ladd for several dramas, including *This Gun for Hire* (1942).

Lake lived here in the early 1940s. Shortly after she married director Andre DeToth in 1944, the couple relocated from this house just outside of Beverly Hills to a farm in the San Fernando Valley community of Chatsworth.

Barbara La Marr (1896–1926)
6672½ Whitley Terrace, Whitley Heights

Barbara La Marr was a silent-era femme fatale who was known as "The Girl Who Is Too Beautiful." La Marr made more than two-dozen movies, including the Douglas Fairbanks blockbuster, *The Three Musketeers* (1921), before succumbing to tuberculosis at age 30. La Marr's show business career includes an early stint as a screenwriter for Fox films under the name Folly Lytell.

In addition to this house in the historic Whitley Heights district, La Marr owned a beach house in Malibu. The Malibu house was literally blown up in the 1965 movie, *Inside Daisy Clover*.

Hedy Lamarr (1913–2000)
1802 Angelo Drive, Beverly Hills

Austrian-born Hedy Lamarr was lauded more for her beauty than her acting skills. Lamarr's brief nude scenes in the German movie, *Ecstasy* (1933), caught the eye of Hollywood moguls. Her best-known role is that of Delilah, opposite Victor Mature, in *Samson and Delilah* (1949). Beyond acting, Lamarr is also known for co-inventing a torpedo guidance system used in World War II. She said that her interest in the field had been piqued by her first husband's work as a munitions manufacturer.

Lamarr moved into this Spanish-style Beverly Hills house in the early 1940s. Among her other homes was a clapboard farmhouse near Beverly Hills, which she called Hedgerow (2707 Benedict Canyon Drive—see Ann-Margret). Her mother once quipped that Lamarr—who was married six times—changed houses as often as she changed husbands.

Hedy Lamarr
1802 Angelo Drive, Beverly Hills

Dorothy Lamour (1914–1996)
9131 Calle Juela Drive, Beverly Hills

Dorothy Lamour was a radio singer when she landed the lead in her first movie, *The Jungle Princess* (1936). It was the first of many roles in which she would wear some form of beach attire. That trend continued with the six popular "Road" movies she made with Bing Crosby and Bob Hope.

From 1947 until the early 1950s, Lamour lived with her husband and their two sons in this modified Georgian-style house above Trousdale Estates.

Elsa Lanchester (1902–1986)
1825 North Curson Avenue, Hollywood Hills

Elsa Lanchester played many colorful supporting roles throughout her career, but she is most closely identified with the big-haired, young bride who greets Boris Karloff with a hiss in *Bride of Frankenstein* (1935). Lanchester later appeared in such movies as *The Big Clock* (1948), *Witness for the Prosecution* (1957) and *Bell Book and Candle* (1958).

Lanchester lived here for more than 30 years, starting in the early 1950s when she and her husband, actor Charles Laughton, relocated from Pacific Palisades to this tile-roofed house in the Hollywood Hills. When the couple first arrived in Hollywood in the early 1930s, Lanchester observed, "Everybody's house seems to be a kind of personal wish-fulfillment."

Charles Laughton (1899–1962)
1825 North Curson Avenue, Hollywood Hills

Charles Laughton was adept at playing moody or tortured souls in films such as *Payment Deferred* (1932), *Mutiny on the Bounty* (1935) and *The Hunchback of Notre Dame* (1939). In 1933 he won the Academy Award for Best Actor for his performance in *The Private Life of Henry VIII* (1933).

This was Laughton's last home. He and his wife, actress Elsa Lanchester, moved to this Lloyd Wright-designed house from Pacific Palisades after a mini landslide in 1949 swept part of their beloved garden into the sea. The erosion was caused by water from a garden hose that had been left running while they were on vacation. Laughton considered the mishap to be a bad omen so they left the house for good.

Stan Laurel (1890–1965)
718 North Bedford Drive, Beverly Hills

Although he played the whimpering, dull-witted member of the Laurel & Hardy team, Stan Laurel supervised the writing and production of most of their films, including the Academy Award-winning, *The Music Box* (1932). In 1917, Laurel sailed to the United States from England along with Charlie Chaplin as part of Fred Karno's vaudeville troupe. Before he paired with Oliver Hardy, Laurel had dozens of supporting roles in dramas and comedies.

Laurel resided in this two-story Beverly Hills house in the early 1930s. He later moved to Canoga Park where, in an effort to discourage curious passersby, he erected a fence in front of his house with a sign that read "Fort Laurel."

Peter Lawford (1923–1984)
625 Palisades Beach Road, Santa Monica

Peter Lawford was a young supporting player during the 1940s, appearing in the likes of *Mrs. Miniver* (1942), *Girl Crazy* (1943) and *The Picture of Dorian Gray* (1945). Lawford began leading a higher-profile life after he married John F. Kennedy's sister, Patricia. Eight years later he co-starred in the original *Ocean's Eleven* (1960).

This house was originally owned by film mogul Louis B. Mayer. Among other accoutrements was a stage located under the floorboards

that could be raised by hydraulic lifts. President John F. Kennedy was Lawford's guest here during the 1960 Democratic National Convention, and used the house later to rendezvous with Marilyn Monroe.

Stan Laurel
718 North Bedford Drive, Beverly Hills

Francis Lederer (1899–2000)
23134 Sherman Way, Canoga Park

Francis Lederer was a Czechoslovakian stage player when he was cast as a Revolutionary War deserter in *Pursuit of Happiness* (1934), starring Joan Bennett. Lederer later starred in *Confessions of a Nazi Spy* (1939) and *Diary of a Chamber Maid* (1946). Lederer died less than six months before his 101st birthday.

The City of Los Angeles declared Lederer's Canoga Park home a Historic-Cultural Monument, calling it a "distinguished example of Mission Revival" architecture. The U-shaped house was originally part of a rambling ranch, which Lederer established in the 1930s (this is a view of the house from Sherman Place, a street near Sherman Way).

Janet Leigh (1927–)
1625 Summitridge Drive, Los Angeles

Although she doesn't stay on screen for long in Alfred Hitchcock's *Psycho* (1960), Janet Leigh's name may be forever linked with that movie. Leigh portrayed a small-time embezzler who winds up at The Bates Motel where she is attacked in the shower by the creepy Norman Bates, played by Anthony Perkins. *Touch of Evil* (1958) and *The Manchurian Candidate* (1962) were among Leigh's other notable films.

Leigh bought this corner estate in 1991. It is surrounded by ivy and trees, and is a far cry from her first Los Angeles home. That was the Harvey

Hotel on Santa Monica Boulevard near Western Avenue, where she lived in the mid-1940s. Leigh later described it as "run-down, sleazy. But the price was right—seven dollars a week for a room and a bath on the third floor."

Jack Lemmon (1925–2001)
10483 Sandal Lane, Bel Air

Jack Lemmon won an Academy Award for Best Supporting Actor for his performance as Ensign Pulver in *Mister Roberts* (1955). Lemmon's many other hits include *Some Like It Hot* (1959), *The Apartment* (1960) and *The Odd Couple* (1968). Lemmon won his second Oscar—this one for Best Actor—for *Save the Tiger* (1973).

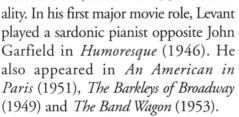

This was Lemmon's home around the time he made *The Apartment* and *The Days of Wine and Roses*. It is located in a pocket of privacy just off of Bel Air Road. At home Lemmon could embody the persnickety character he played in *The Odd Couple*. His wife, Felicia, once commented, "When we were first married, he had to have everything symmetrical and stacked neatly."

Oscar Levant (1906–1972)
905 North Roxbury Drive, Beverly Hills

Concert pianist Oscar Levant started in films by writing musical scores for silent movies. He appeared in a few silent features, and in the 1930s became a radio personality. In his first major movie role, Levant played a sardonic pianist opposite John Garfield in *Humoresque* (1946). He also appeared in *An American in Paris* (1951), *The Barkleys of Broadway* (1949) and *The Band Wagon* (1953).

Levant and his family lived here in the mid-1960s. When he came to California in 1947 to make *Romance on the High Seas* (1948), Levant rented a house on Camden Drive that was located just across the alley from Gene Kelly, with whom he would appear in two hit movies several years later.

Beatrice Lillie (1894–1989)
Chateau Marmont
8221 West Sunset Boulevard, West Hollywood

Beginning in 1914, Beatrice Lillie, known for her ever-present cigarette holder, performed her own witty stage review in London and on Broadway for several decades. She eventually took her act to radio and then movies, appearing in *Exit Smiling* (1926), *Around the World in Eighty Days* (1956) and *Thoroughly Modern Millie* (1967).

Lillie lived at the Chateau Marmont while shooting *Thoroughly Modern Mille*. She is one of scores of actors who have lived at the hotel for extended periods.

Harold Lloyd (1893–1971)
502 South Irving Boulevard, Los Angeles
443 Palisades Beach Road, Santa Monica

The bespectacled screen character that Harold Lloyd created in 1917 became one of the darlings of the silent era. Lloyd's character, known for dangling from skyscrapers, invariably became entangled in silly misunderstandings. *Safety Last* (1923) and *The Freshman* (1925) were among his most lauded features. In 1952 Lloyd received a special Oscar for his contributions to filmmaking.

502 South Irving Boulevard: Right after Lloyd and actress Mildred Davis married in 1923, they moved to this Italianate-style house. They lived here until 1928 when their famous Greenacres estate in Beverly Hills was completed.

443 Palisades Beach Road: The Lloyds owned this beach house on Santa Monica's Gold Coast during the 1930s. The house was just steps away from Marion Davies' popular beachfront estate.

Harold Lloyd
502 South Irving Boulevard, Los Angeles

Carole Lombard (1908–1942)
4543 Tara Drive, Encino

Carole Lombard gained fame by playing tart-mouthed women in such screwball comedies as *Twentieth Century* (1934) opposite John Barrymore, *My Man Godfrey* (1936) with ex-husband William Powell and *Nothing Sacred* (1937) with Fredric March. Lombard's career was in full swing when she was killed in a plane crash during a war bond drive in 1942.

In the late 1930s, Lombard and her husband, Clark Gable, bought a 20-acre ranch in Encino. What was once the ranch is today an upscale housing tract that includes the residence behind this gate, which was Gable and Lombard's original ranch house. Lombard once quipped, "It's the most elegant shithouse in the San Fernando Valley."

Peter Lorre (1904–1964)
7655 Hollywood Boulevard, Hollywood

During the 1930s and 1940s, when a director needed to cast a dark, offbeat character, Peter Lorre was frequently at the top of the list. Lorre's often-imitated voice sounded like he was speaking through his nose. He was memorable in *The Man Who Knew Too Much* (1934), *Crime and Punishment* (1935), *The Maltese Falcon* (1941) and *Casablanca* (1942).

After separating from his third wife in 1962, Lorre moved from their Beverly Hills-area home to a two-bedroom apartment in this Hollywood Boulevard building.

Peter Lorre
7655 Hollywood Boulevard, Hollywood

❖

Myrna Loy (1905–1993)
9551 Hidden Valley Road, Los Angeles

Myrna Loy's first movie role was a bit part in *What Price Beauty* (filmed in 1925, released in 1928). She was then cast as an Asian woman in several movies before appearing opposite William Powell in *Manhattan Melodrama* (1934). Impressed with the duo's on-screen chemistry, MGM cast them as the droll Nora and Nick Charles in *The Thin Man* (1934)

and several sequels. Loy's other memorable films include *Test Pilot* (1938) and *The Best Years of Our Lives* (1946).

In the late 1930s, Loy and her husband, producer Arthur Hornblow, built this house in an undeveloped area near the top of Coldwater Canyon. After they moved in they discovered that Boris Karloff was a neighbor. Loy wrote in her memoir, "We knew that Boris Karloff lived somewhere above us because his bowling green wasn't properly engineered and the balls kept tumbling down the mountain."

Bela Lugosi (1882–1956)
1146 North Hudson Avenue, Hollywood

Little did Bela Lugosi know that when he reprised his Broadway role as Dracula in the 1931 film of the same name, he'd be permanently identified with the title character. Lugosi's image as a horror flick king was reinforced by the studios, who insisted on typecasting him in scores of similar roles. After *Dracula*, one of Lugosi's most popular films was *Son of Frankenstein* (1939), in

which he was paired with Boris Karloff of *Frankenstein* fame.

Even after *Dracula* made Lugosi a star in the early 1930s, he continued renting this simple Hollywood bungalow.

Ida Lupino (1914–1995)
13211 Old Oak Lane, Brentwood

Ida Lupino, who once joked that she was the poor man's Bette Davis, was best known for playing tough, stubborn women in movies like *They Drive by Night* (1940), *High Sierra* (1941) and *The Hard Way* (1942). In 1949, Lupino began adding producing, directing and writing credits to her resume—a rarity for a woman at that time. Among her most financially successful directing efforts was *The Trouble with Angels* (1966), starring Haley Mills.

Lupino had many homes during her career, including two in Brentwood. She lived in this home during the 1960s. During the mid-1940s, Lupino lived alone for nearly a year on a small yacht in Newport Beach, California.

Jeanette MacDonald (1903–1965)
621 North Bedford Drive, Beverly Hills

A soprano who also had a screen presence, Jeanette MacDonald was paired first with Maurice Chevalier for three light comedies, and then with baritone Nelson Eddy. She and Eddy starred in such movies as *Naughty Marietta* (1935), *Rose-Marie* (1936) and *Maytime* (1937).

Around 1930, MacDonald moved out of what is now known as the Regent Beverly Wilshire Hotel (9500 Wilshire Boulevard—see Warren Beatty and Lon Chaney) and into this rented house on Bedford. She liked to maintain her suntan by lying on the swimming pool diving board.

Shirley MacLaine (1934–)
4001 Royal Oak Place, Encino

Shirley MacLaine was considered one of Hollywood's most talented young stars when she appeared as the love struck elevator operator in *The Apartment* (1960). Her subsequent movies include *The Children's Hour* (1961), *Sweet Charity* (1969) and *Being There* (1979). MacLaine earned the Best Actress Oscar for her performance as Debra Winger's difficult mother in *Terms of Endearment* (1983).

MacLaine lived in this Encino home during the 1960s. From the street, visitors can see the driveway surrounded by trees and a bed of ivy, but the house itself isn't visible. When she came to Los Angeles for the first time in the mid-1950s (to film *The Trouble with Harry*), MacLaine and her husband, producer Steve Parker, leased a one-room apartment in Malibu.

Fred MacMurray (1908–1991)
485 Halvern Drive, Brentwood

Among Fred MacMurray's most popular movie roles were Katharine Hepburn's love interest in *Alice Adams* (1935) and Barbara Stanwyck's partner in crime in *Double Indemnity* (1944). MacMurray also appeared in *The Egg and I* (1947) and several other features with Claudette Colbert. In the 1960s he starred in the TV series *My Three Sons* (1960–1972).

MacMurray's Brentwood house was built by singer/actor Nelson Eddy in 1938. It is a replica of the Colonial-style houses found in Williamsburg, Virginia, where Eddy grew up.

Dorothy Malone (1925–)
713 North Beverly Drive, Beverly Hills

Dorothy Malone was a fixture in the top melodramas of the 1950s, including *Written on the Wind* (1956), in which her portrayal of the heiress who sets her sites on Rock Hudson earned her the Oscar for Best Actress. Malone can also be seen in *Sincerely Yours* (1955), *Man of a Thousand Faces* (1957) and *Too Much Too Soon* (1958).

Malone was one of Hollywood's top stars when she resided in this well-hidden mansion just south of Sunset.

Herbert Marshall (1890–1966)
716 North Rexford Drive, Beverly Hills

Herbert Marshall was among the many British actors who were recruited by Hollywood in the 1930s and 1940s. Among his comedies were Ernst Lubitsch's *Trouble in Paradise* (1932), in which he romances both Miriam Hopkins and Kay Francis. His dramatic roles include the husband who Bette Davis tries to coldly manipulate in *The Little Foxes* (1941).

Marshall lived in this French Traditional-style house during the 1940s, when he appeared in some of his most popular movies, including *The Razor's Edge* (1946).

The Marx Brothers

The Marx Brothers brought a new kind of comic chaos to the movies. Chico, with his fake Italian accent, played the conman; wisecracking Groucho played the chief instigator of the brothers' schemes; curly-top Harpo was the silent, mischievous one; and Zeppo, who appeared in only six of the Marx Brothers movies, invariably played the straight man.

Chico Marx (1887–1961)
724 North Elm Drive, Beverly Hills

Chico Marx and his family lived in this Elm Drive house in the 1940s. In the early 1930s, shortly after he arrived in California, Chico rented a hillside house that

was later owned by George Burns and Gracie Allen.

Groucho Marx (1890–1977)
1083 Hillcrest Road, Beverly Hills

This Trousdale Estates house was home to Groucho Marx well into the 1970s. Among his previous homes was a two-story, 16-room Beverly Hills villa, complete

with a citrus orchard. He moved out in the 1950s after divorcing his third wife.

Harpo Marx (1888–1964)
701 North Canon Drive, Beverly Hills

Harpo Marx rented this mansion completely furnished in the 1940s. He lived at the Garden of Allah during his early Hollywood years.

Zeppo Marx (1901–1979)
907 North Bedford Drive, Beverly Hills

Zeppo Marx resided here during the mid-1930s. While the Marx Bros. were still getting established in Hollywood, Zeppo had an apartment on Havenhurst in Hollywood and a beach cottage in Malibu.

James Mason (1909–1984)
1018 Pamela Drive, Beverly Hills

James Mason was a debonair leading man in British dramas for a decade before relocating to Hollywood in the late 1940s. He won over American audiences in such films as *Julius Caesar* (1953), *A Star Is Born* (1954) and *North by Northwest* (1959).

Buster Keaton built the Italian Renaissance-style mansion beyond these gates in 1925. Mason and his wife, television and radio personality

Pamela Mason, bought it in 1949. Seven years later they discovered a stash of Keaton films—including some that film historians assumed had been lost forever—locked in a safe that was stored in a tool shed on the property.

Raymond Massey (1896–1983)
913 North Beverly Drive, Beverly Hills

Fans of historical dramas know Raymond Massey for his powerful performance as Abe Lincoln in *Abe Lincoln in Illinois* (1940). Massey also played the strange Jonathan Brewster in *Arsenic and Old Lace* (1944), and James Dean's father in *East of Eden* (1955).

After living in Connecticut for many years, Massey and his wife, Dorothy, moved to this house in Beverly Hills in 1959. Massey wrote in his memoir, "We looked native in a conventional Beverly Hills way, but only on the outside. When Dorothy had finished with the move, installing books and our antique English furniture, the inside became that lovely kind of home she always made for us back east."

Raymond Massey
913 North Beverly Drive, Beverly Hills

Walter Matthau (1920–2000)
278 Toyopa Drive, Pacific Palisades

Walter Matthau began his film career playing dour characters in movies like *A Face in the Crowd* (1957). He finally got a chance at comedy a few years later, playing the phony CIA agent in *Charade* (1963), and Jack Lemmon's slimy brother-in-law in *The Fortune Cookie* (1966), a role which earned Matthau the Academy Award for Best Supporting Actor. He may be best known for playing the slovenly Oscar Madison in *The Odd Couple* (1968).

When Matthau moved from New York to Beverly Hills in 1968, he sublet a house from Paul Newman and Joanne Woodward. Shortly thereafter, his friend, actor William Schallert, convinced him to move to this Pacific Palisades house where he could enjoy the ocean air.

Victor Mature (1913–1999)
205 South Camden Drive, Beverly Hills

Although he was a mostly stoic presence on screen, Victor Mature managed to get cast in a variety of genres. These include the film noir-ish *I Wake Up Screaming* (1941), the Western *My Darling Clementine* (1946), the musical comedy *Footlight Serenade* (1942) and his biggest hit, the romantic drama *Samson and Delilah* (1949).

Mature's career was starting to look promising when he lived in this Beverly Hills house located south of Wilshire. He later retired to an estate in Rancho Santa Fe, California, just north of San Diego.

Walter Matthau
278 Toyopa Drive, Pacific Palisades

Hattie McDaniel (1895–1952)
2203 South Harvard Boulevard, Los Angeles

Hattie McDaniel became the first black performer to earn an Academy Award when she won the Best Supporting Actress Oscar for her portrayal of the stalwart, mischievous Mammy in *Gone With the Wind* (1939). The versatile McDaniel had singing parts in *Show Boat* (1936) and later *Song of the South* (1946).

McDaniel decorated the interior of this home in a Chinese theme. She kept her Oscar in the music room. McDaniel bought the property in 1941. Some of her white neighbors filed a lawsuit claiming that a "restrictive covenant" prevented the home from being sold to a black person. McDaniel led a fight against the lawsuit, which was thrown out a few years later.

Roddy McDowall (1928–1998)
3110 Brookdale Road, Studio City

Roddy McDowall was just 10 years old when he won his first movie role in his native England. After three years and many more movies, McDowall was brought to Hollywood by director John Ford to play the youngest son of a Welsh coal miner in *How Green Was My Valley* (1941). His other films include *Lassie Come Home* (1943), *Cleopatra* (1963) and *Funny Lady* (1975).

McDowall lived across the street from Gene Autry's long-time home. His house was filled with movie memorabilia, including his collection of vintage movie magazines and movie posters.

Hattie McDaniel
2203 South Harvard Boulevard, Los Angeles

Darren McGavin (1922–)
713 North Canon Drive, Beverly Hills

Sandy-haired Darren McGavin's varied big screen roles included a drug dealer in *The Man With the Golden Arm* (1955), Jerry Lewis' comic partner in *The Delicate*

Delinquent (1957) and Adam Sandler's father in *Billy Madison* (1995).

This was McGavin's home in the mid-1960s. Located in one of the first residential districts in Beverly Hills, the house was built in 1911. Today it has a Neo-French design.

Dorothy McGuire (1916–2001)
121 Copley Place, Beverly Hills

Dorothy McGuire's niche was playing the wholesome, supportive mother and wife. In one of her first movie roles she played the patient mother, Katie Nolan, in *A Tree Grows in Brooklyn* (1945). Twenty years later McGuire portrayed the Virgin Mary in *The Greatest Story Ever Told* (1965). She also co-starred in *Gentleman's Agreement* (1947) opposite Gregory Peck and *Friendly Persuasion* (1956) opposite Gary Cooper.

McGuire lived on this estate from the 1950s. Adjacent to the Los Angeles Country Club, it is in the secluded Copley Place neighborhood south of Sunset.

Dorothy McGuire
121 Copley Place, Beverly Hills

Steve McQueen (1930–1980)
2419 Solar Drive, Hollywood Hills

Following years of minor film roles, Steve McQueen's performance in *The Magnificent Seven* (1960) proved to be a turning point. He went on to achieve superstar status with *The Great Escape* (1963). McQueen also starred in *Bullitt* (1968), *The Getaway* (1972) and *Papillon* (1973).

In 1960, McQueen bought this sprawling, Japanese-style house located high atop a Nichols Canyon hill. Three years later McQueen moved his family to a compound in Brentwood. At the time, McQueen said,

"I have a very tight-knit family, but you've got to build a wall around them to keep people out because the world is full of phonies. It's important for people like me to have sanctuary and privacy. "

Adolphe Menjou (1890–1963)
722 North Bedford Drive, Beverly Hills

Adolphe Menjou added a dash of sophistication and wit to the movies in which he appeared. Menjou was featured alongside Rudolph Valentino in *The Sheik* (1921) and Douglas Fairbanks in *The Three Musketeers* (1921). He went on to co-star in many more hits, from *The Front Page* (1931) to *Paths of Glory* (1957). Off-screen, Menjou was frequently named America's best-dressed man.

In 1924, someone advised Menjou to avoid Beverly Hills because he'd have to face the sun's glare while driving to and from work. Menjou ended up building two houses above Los Feliz. Then, according to Menjou in his memoir, "In 1939, I bought a pair of dark glasses and built a house in Beverly Hills."

Bette Midler (1945–)
9481 Readcrest Drive, Los Angeles

Bette Midler entered show business with a cabaret-style stage act in New York. She earned an Academy Award nomination for her performance as a tormented rock

singer in *The Rose* (1979), one of her first movie roles. Midler went on to co-star in such major hits as *Down and Out in Beverly Hills* (1986), *Beaches* (1988) and *First Wives' Club* (1996).

Midler bought this Mediterranean-style Coldwater Canyon-area estate in the 1980s. Contemplating her home life, Midler once said, "This house is like a canvas to me. I have a nesting instinct that didn't come out until I bought [the house] and now seems to be overwhelming me."

Ray Milland (1905–1986)
726 North Elm Drive, Beverly Hills

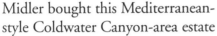

Ray Milland may be best remembered for his Academy Award-winning portrayal of an alcoholic in Billy Wilder's *Lost Weekend* (1945). Milland, whose career began as a dancer in England, also starred in *Dial M for Murder* (1954), as well as the Bing Crosby-Carole Lombard comedy, *We're Not Dressing* (1934). In 1970 Milland played Ryan O'Neal's father in *Love Story*.

Milland and his wife, Mal, built this Tudor-style house in the early 1940s. Their interior decorator was Gladys Belzer, Loretta Young's mother.

Ann Miller (1923–2004)
618 North Alta Drive, Beverly Hills

Ann Miller's energetic tap dancing won her many roles in movies that were heavier on music than acting. But Miller also was called on for light comedies, *You Can't Take It with You* (1938), as well as *Easter Parade* (1948), where she kept pace with Fred Astaire. In 2001 Miller had a small part in David Lynch's eccentric drama, *Mulholland Dr.*

Miller moved from a Benedict Canyon residence into this house after splitting with her husband, Arthur Cameron, in 1962. She lived here with her mother and her French poodle, Poochie. Miller originally bought the house for her mother.

Yvette Mimieux (1942–)
9854 Portola Drive, Los Angeles

Yvette Mimieux's first role in a major movie was the futuristic Weena in *The Time Machine* (1960). Her later roles include a rape victim in *Where the Boys Are* (1960), a troubled bride in *Joy in the Morning* (1965) and an inmate in *Jackson County Jail* (1976).

This was Mimieux's home in the 1960s. The house was built in 1922 and substantially renovated in 1930.

Ann Miller
618 North Alta Drive, Beverly Hills

Sal Mineo (1939–1976)
8565 Holloway Drive, West Hollywood

His heart-rending performance as the innocent Plato in *Rebel Without a Cause* (1955) made Sal Mineo a star almost overnight. He appeared again with James Dean in *Giant* (1956), then played the lead in *The Gene Krupa Story* (1959), and had an important supporting role in *Exodus* (1960).

Mineo was murdered at the age of 37 outside of this apartment complex. Police later determined it was a random killing.

Mary Miles Minter (1902–1984)
144 Adelaide Drive, Santa Monica

Mary Miles Minter played innocent waifs in silent films such as *Anne of Green Gables* (1919), but her name was sullied in 1922 when she became intertwined in the controversy surrounding the murder that year of director William Desmond Taylor. Minter wasn't a suspect, but many believe that her mother committed the crime, which has never been solved. Minter's last movie was in 1923.

After leaving the movies behind, Minter moved to Beverly Hills. She eventually settled in this house in the Palisades section of Santa Monica. In 1981 Minter was robbed and nearly beaten to death in this house.

Mary Miles Minter
144 Adelaide Drive, Santa Monica

Robert Mitchum (1917–1997)
314 Wisconsin Avenue, Long Beach
3372 Oak Glen Drive, Los Angeles

Robert Mitchum spent much of his career portraying cool studs and street toughs. His performance as a hardened military officer opposite Burgess Meredith in *The Story of G.I. Joe* (1945) earned Mitchum an Academy Award nomination. He also distinguished himself in *Thirty Seconds Over Tokyo* (1944), *The Night of the Hunter* (1955) and *Cape Fear* (1962 and 1991).

314 Wisconsin Avenue: Mitchum was a teenager when he lived with his parents and siblings in this Long Beach cottage during the early 1930s. He got his first taste of acting at the nearby Players Guild in Long Beach.

3372 Oak Glen Drive: In the late 1940s Mitchum, now an established star, settled with his young family into this house near Universal Studios.

Tom Mix (1880–1940)
1614 Golden Gate Avenue, Silver Lake

Tom Mix learned to handle a horse and wield a lasso during his years as a rodeo star. When he turned to acting in 1910, Mix created a new brand of Western star— a flamboyantly dressed man of action and humor. He and his savvy horse, Tony, starred in numerous hits, including *The Lone Star Ranger* (1923) and *Riders of the Purple Sage* (1925). Mix appeared in only a few talkies before leaving Hollywood to perform in a circus which he produced himself.

In 1918, Mix lived in this house located in Los Angeles' Silver Lake neighborhood. Nearby was Mixville, the special Fox studio lot where Mix's films were produced from 1917 to 1925.

Marilyn Monroe (1926–1962)
El Palacio Apartments
8491–8499 Fountain Avenue, West Hollywood
Avalon Hotel
9400 West Olympic Boulevard, Beverly Hills

After a series of bit parts (most notably 1950's *All About Eve*), Marilyn Monroe landed her first starring role when she was cast as a homicidal bride in *Niagara* (1953). What followed were mostly comic parts in which she played variations on the seductive lost soul, in such hits as *Gentlemen Prefer Blondes* (1953), *The Seven Year Itch* (1955) and *Some Like It Hot* (1959). Monroe's last completed film, the drama *The Misfits* (1961), was also Clark Gable's final film. Both were lauded for their perceptive performances.

8491–8499 Fountain Avenue: Monroe was starting to get small movie roles when she lived at the El Palacio Apartments in the late 1940s. Monroe, who led a nomadic life as a child, would continue to move every few years throughout most of her life.

9400 West Olympic Boulevard: In the early 1950s, Monroe moved into an apartment at the Beverly Carlton Hotel (now called the Avalon Hotel). Among the few personal items she brought with her were her books and a picture of stage actress Eleonora Duse. After Monroe moved out she kept the apartment so she could continue receiving her mail there.

Marilyn Monroe
El Palacio Apartments, 8491–8499 Fountain Avenue, West Hollywood

George Montgomery (1916–2000)
400 Drury Lane, Beverly Hills

During the 1940s, George Montgomery portrayed unruffled leading men in such movies as *Roxie Hart* (1942) with Ginger Rogers and *Coney Island* (1943) with Betty Grable. Following World War II, he appeared in Westerns such as *The Pathfinder* (1952) and *The Toughest Gun in Tombstone* (1958).

Montgomery lived in this house during the 1950s. One of Montgomery's favorite pastimes was building houses and designing furniture. Beginning in the 1940s, Montgomery built and sold several spacious homes in the San Fernando Valley and Beverly Hills. When he put one of his Beverly Hills estates on the market in 1985, Montgomery, a travel buff, told *The Los Angeles Times*, "The house just ties me down."

Robert Montgomery (1904–1981)
506 North Bedford Drive, Beverly Hills

Robert Montgomery played many a ladies' man in movies like *Their Own Desire* (1930) and *No More Ladies* (1935). But audiences also found him con-

vincing as a psychopathic killer in *Night Must Fall* (1937), and as the boxer who is surprised to find himself dead in the light comedy *Here Comes Mr. Jordan* (1941).

Spruce trees line the house where Montgomery lived in the early 1950s. He later lived in Holmby Hills, then moved to New York.

Colleen Moore (1900–1988)
1119 South Grand View Street, Los Angeles

The defining moment in Colleen Moore's career came in 1923 when she starred as a rebellious flapper in *Flaming Youth*. Her daring Dutch bob haircut in that film is credited with fueling the hairstyle's popularity among teenage girls of the 1920s. Moore later played more serious roles in such films as *So Big* (1924) and *Lilac Time* (1928).

Moore resided here in the early 1920s. Moore later bought a Bel Air estate (321 Saint Pierre Road—see Robert Stack). In her memoir, Moore recalled of the mansions of the day, "We splurged on homes partly because our intensive work schedules didn't permit such luxuries as travel, partly because what started out as necessities or conveniences became status symbols, and partly because most of us had more money than sense."

Agnes Moorehead (1900–1974)
1023 North Roxbury Drive, Beverly Hills

Agnes Moorehead honed her acting skills as part of Orson Welles' Mercury Theater company. Her first movie role was the small part of Welles' mother in *Citizen Kane* (1941). Moorehead also played the unstable Fanny in *The Magnificent Ambersons* (1942), and had major supporting roles in *Dark Passage* (1947) and *Hush…Hush, Sweet Charlotte* (1964). All this was before Moorehead played Samantha's mother in TV's *Bewitched* (1964-1972).

Moorehead named this U-shaped house Villa Agnese. On Sundays it wasn't unusual for Moorehead to spend the entire day on her terrace patio.

Frank Morgan (1890–1949)
1025 Ridgedale Drive, Beverly Hills

Frank Morgan, one of the busiest character actors of Hollywood's golden age, is still beloved throughout the world for his role as the befuddled wizard in the *Wizard of Oz* (1939). Morgan also co-starred in hits like *The Great Ziegfeld* (1936), *The Shop Around the Corner* (1940) and *Boom Town* (1940). Morgan was working on a New Mexico ranch in 1919 when his brother, actor Ralph Morgan, convinced him to try acting.

This elegant, white mansion—fitting for any wizard—was Morgan's home while he made *The Wizard of Oz* and other hits of the era. The house is directly across the street from the estate that today belongs to Brad Pitt and Jennifer Aniston.

Robert Morse (1931–)
325 Avondale Avenue, Brentwood

Famous for his lively performances as well as the gap between his front teeth, Robert Morse became a hot property in Hollywood after his Tony Award-winning performance on Broadway in *How to Succeed in Business Without Really Trying*. He played the same part in the 1967 movie version of the play. Morse also co-starred in *A Guide for the Married Man* (1967) and *The Boatniks* (1970), before devoting his time to the stage and television.

A sizeable front lawn and a tall hedge put a considerable distance between Morse's house and Avondale Avenue. He lived in this Brentwood residence when his hit movie, *How to Succeed in Business Without Really Trying*, was released.

Alan Mowbray (1896–1969)
1019 Chevy Chase Drive, Beverly Hills

Alan Mowbray refined the art of portraying the snobbish Englishman in both dramas and comedies. He carried himself with an imperious air throughout his 30-year career in movies, including *Becky Sharp* (1935), *My Man Godfrey* (1936), *Topper* (1937) and *The King and I* (1956).

Mowbray lived in this Chevy Chase Drive house while making such movies as *My Man Godfrey* and *Topper*. Greta Garbo lived on the same block.

Eddie Murphy (1961–)
2727 Benedict Canyon Drive, Los Angeles

Eddie Murphy was just 19 when he joined the ensemble at TV's *Saturday Night Live*. Two years later he co-starred with Nick Nolte in *48 Hours* (1982). He went on to star

in one of the biggest moneymakers in motion picture history, *Beverly Hills Cop* (1984). Over the years, Murphy has showcased his versatility by playing multiple characters. In *The Nutty Professor* (1996) he portrayed seven characters.

In the late 1980s, Murphy bought this Benedict Canyon home once owned by Cher. His Egyptian-style house behind these gates stands on four acres.

George Murphy (1902–1992)
807 North Rodeo Drive, Beverly Hills

From the early 1930s, George Murphy, already an accomplished dancer, appeared in musicals such as *Broadway Melody of 1938* (1937) and *For Me and My Gal* (1942). Murphy was elected a U.S. Senator from California in 1965 and held the post until 1971.

Murphy once hired interior-decorator-to-the-stars, Billy Haines, to decorate one of his homes. Murphy later recalled being shocked by

the price tag of one of Haines' first purchases for the house—$1,000 for an antique secretary desk. Haines convinced him that it was money well spent, even for an actor who had yet to become a movie star.

Carmel Myers (1899–1980)
621 North Arden Drive, Beverly Hills

The smoky-eyed Carmel Myers starred opposite Rudolph Valentino in *Society Sensation* (1918) and Ramon Novarro and Francis X. Bushman in *Ben-Hur* (1925). Myers continued to work in the talkies and later went on to television, where she hosted a live talk show in the early 1950s.

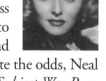

Myers and her husband, Ralph Blum, were the original owners of this Arden Drive house, which was built in 1924. The home featured a solarium, a library and a swimming pool. Many years later, Myers moved into the Colonial House (1416 North Havenhurst Drive—see Bette Davis).

Patricia Neal (1926–)
2146 Fox Hills Drive, Los Angeles

Patricia Neal earned an Academy Award for Best Actress for her portrayal of the housekeeper who is drawn to Paul Newman in *Hud* (1963). Two years later, Neal had a series of strokes that left her severely disabled. Despite the odds, Neal recovered and resumed her career, starring in *The Subject Was Roses* (1968), among other films.

Neal's lengthy affair with Gary Cooper (her co-star in three movies) was well known in Hollywood. The two would meet at this Los Angeles apartment where Neal lived during the 1950s.

Paul Newman (1925–)
1117 Tower Road, Beverly Hills

Paul Newman's reputation as an actor's actor took shape during his years on the New York stage. But it was his portrayal of boxer Rocky Graziano in *Somebody Up There Likes Me* (1956), that brought him acclaim in Hollywood. Newman's other classics have included *Long Hot Summer* (1958) with Joanne Woodward (who would become his wife in 1958); *Cat on a Hot Tin Roof* (1958), *Hud* (1963), two blockbusters with Robert Redford—*Butch Cassidy and the Sundance Kid* (1969) and *The Sting* (1973)—and *The Color of Money* (1986).

Newman and Woodward, who stay in the Hollywood area while filming movies, lived here in the early 1960s, but they have always preferred living on the East Coast. In 1961, they bought a house in Connecticut so that their kids could grow up away from the Hollywood scene.

Jack Nicholson (1937–)
12850 Mulholland Drive, Los Angeles

His trademark Cheshire-cat grin and bad-boy image define Jack Nicholson's film persona. He delivered memorable performances in such box office hits as *Carnal Knowledge* (1971) and *Chinatown* (1974), and earned Oscars for his roles in *One Flew Over the Cukoo's Nest* (1975), *Terms of Endearment* (1983), and *As Good as It Gets* (1999).

Nicholson's house is tucked away off of Mulholland. He has lived here for at least two decades. Marlon Brando and Warren Beatty live nearby. Mulholland has become known as "Bad Boy Drive" because of the notorious actors who live, and have lived, on the street.

Paul Newman
1117 Tower Road, Beverly Hills

Anna Q. Nilsson (1888–1974)
438 South Doheny Drive, Beverly Hills

Anna Q. Nilsson first stepped before a movie camera in 1911 when she starred in the one-reeler *Molly Pitcher*. The Nordic beauty was featured in more than 50 silent films. In 1925, Nilsson suffered serious injuries when she was thrown from a horse. After taking a year off to recover, she made a

few more movies, including *The Babe Comes Home* (1927), in which she co-starred with baseball legend Babe Ruth. Nilsson later had small, uncredited roles in major movies such as *Sunset Boulevard* (1950), *An American In Paris* (1951) and *Seven Brides for Seven Brothers* (1954).

In the 1940s, Nilsson settled here on the southern edge of Beverly Hills. A long-time Beverly Hills resident, she lived on North Crescent Drive in the 1930s.

David Niven (1909–1983)
1461 Amalfi Drive, Pacific Palisades

David Niven played amiable British military men and *bon vivants* in movies such as *The Dawn Patrol* (1938) and the blockbuster, *Around the World in Eighty Days* (1956). He won the Academy Award for Best Actor for his performance in *Separate Tables* (1958). Nine years later he portrayed James Bond in *Casino Royale* (1967). Author Ian Fleming said that David Niven had been his model for the James Bond character.

This became known as "The Pink House" when Niven lived here because the house and the surrounding walls were painted pale pink (they still are today). Niven lived in the Pink House until the early 1960s, then moved to Switzerland.

Nick Nolte (1941–)
6173 Bonsall Drive, Malibu

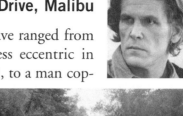

Nick Nolte's most significant roles have ranged from his comic performance as a homeless eccentric in *Down and Out in Beverly Hills* (1986), to a man coping with his troubled family in *The Prince of Tides* (1991). Nolte also earned positive reviews for *Affliction* (1997), in which he played a sheriff whose mental health unravels while he investigates a murder involving a friend.

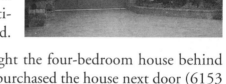

In the fall of 1991, Nolte bought the four-bedroom house behind this gate. Two months later he purchased the house next door (6153 Bonsall Drive) along with some of its furnishings.

Mabel Normand (1892–1930)
526 North Camden Drive, Beverly Hills

Mable Normand was an immediate audience favorite when she began appearing in Mack Sennett comedies in 1912. Normand went on to star in such popular features as *The Slim Princess* (1920) and *Molly 'O* (1921). In 1916 she established her own production company. Although it was a short-lived company, it was a trailblazing effort for an actress.

In the mid-1920s, Normand bought her first home—this two-story stucco house—in a Beverly Hills neighborhood where many of her colleagues were also setting up housekeeping.

Kim Novak (1933–)
1215 Lodi Place, Hollywood

Frequently described as an "icy" blonde, Kim Novak's first substantial film role was in *The Pushover* (1954) with Fred MacMurray. She went on to shine in such fifties classics as *Picnic* (1955) and the Alfred Hitchcock thriller *Vertigo* (1958) in which she played two roles opposite James Stewart. Novak retired from the screen in 1991.

Early in her career, Novak lived in this building, which was then the YWCA's Hollywood Studio Club. It was founded in 1916 at a different location to provide a safe home for young actresses. Other residents who later became famous include ZaSu Pitts, Marilyn Monroe and Donna Reed.

Ramon Novarro (1899–1968)
5609 Valley Oak Drive, Hollywood Hills

Mexico native Ramon Novarro was one of the most magnetic of the silent era's leading men. His popularity shot through the roof after he played the title role in *Ben-Hur* (1925). When Novarro's star began to dim in the 1930s, he left the United States to make foreign-language movies. He returned to Hollywood in the late 1940s and appeared in a few more movies before retiring.

Novarro bought this modern, four-level house in the Hollywood Hills in the early 1930s. Known as the Samuel-Novarro house, it has been named a cultural landmark by the city of Los Angeles. Novarro sold the Lloyd Wright-designed house in the 1940s. Several decades later, actress Diane Keaton bought it, commenting that she was drawn to the house's "mazelike feeling."

Ramon Novarro
5609 Valley Oak Drive, Hollywood Hills

Jack Oakie (1903–1978)
18605 Devonshire Street, Northridge

Jack Oakie played scores of well-meaning oafs in movies such as *If I Had a Million* (1932) starring Gary Cooper. Oakie is also remembered as Clark Gable's buddy in *The Call of the Wild* (1935) and as a nutty version of Mussolini in Charlie Chaplin's *The Great Dictator* (1940). Oakie had

an ongoing feud with cameramen because he refused to wear makeup in front of the camera.

Oakie purchased this estate, known as Oakridge, from Barbara Stanwyck in the late 1930s. Oakie and his wife, Victoria, invited their Hollywood friends to Sunday afternoon salons at the estate. About 25 years after Oakie's death, Victoria donated the estate to USC, whose School of Cinema-Television awards a Jack Oakie Comedy Scholarship every year.

Merle Oberon (1911–1979)
244 Ladera Drive, Holmby Hills

Merle Oberon starred in a number of popular melo-dramas and period films, including *The Private Life of Henry VIII* (1933), *The Scarlet Pimpernel* (1935) and, most famously, *Wuthering Heights* (1939), in which she played the ill-fated Cathy. In her later years, Oberon appeared in *The Oscar* (1966) and *Hotel* (1967).

Oberon divided her time between two homes in Mexico and this one in Holmby Hills. Although there was a staff of servants at each locale, the detail-minded Oberon was personally involved in keeping all of the households in order.

Maureen O'Hara (1920–)
10677 Somma Way, Bel Air

Statuesque and red-haired, Maureen O'Hara made an impact in one of her first starring roles when she played Esmeralda opposite Charles Laughton's Quasimoto in *The Hunchback of Notre Dame* (1939). She went on to co-star in several admired movies, including *Miracle on 34th Street* (1947), *The Quiet Man* (1952) and *The Parent Trap* (1961). O'Hara surfaced from a 20-year retirement to play John Candy's mother in *Only the Lonely* (1991).

O'Hara's former home in Bel Air has a quaint, country cottage look. For many years, O'Hara spent the winter at her home in St. Croix in the Virgin Islands.

Maureen O'Sullivan (1911–1998)
514 North Beverly Drive, Beverly Hills

Maureen O'Sullivan entered the Hollywood spotlight by playing the intrepid Jane opposite Johnny Weissmuller in *Tarzan the Ape Man* (1934). She played Jane in several more Tarzan movies, and also appeared in *The Thin Man* (1934), *David Copperfield* (1935) and *The Big Clock* (1948). Many years later, O'Sullivan, the mother of actress Mia Farrow, played Mia's mother in Woody Allen's *Hannah and Her Sisters* (1986).

O'Sullivan and her husband, director and writer John Farrow, lived in this Spanish-style house in the early 1940s.

Jack Palance (1919–)
1005 Hartford Way, Beverly Hills

Jack Palance may be best known to today's movie audiences as Curly, the grizzled cowboy in *City Slickers* (1991) and *City Slickers II* (1994). He earned an Oscar for Best Supporting Actor for the first film. A former boxer, Palance practically made a career out of playing tough guys, such as the gun-slinging outlaw in *Shane* (1953) who faces off against Alan Ladd in a gun draw.

For several decades, Palance has lived in this house, located just a few blocks north of the Beverly Hills Hotel.

Eleanor Parker (1922–)
620 North Beverly Drive, Beverly Hills

One of many leading-ladies that Hollywood cultivated in the 1940s, Eleanor Parker appeared in several war-related movies before earning Oscar nominations for *Caged* (1950), *Detective Story* (1951) and *Interrupted Melody* (1955). She also co-starred in two of Frank Sinatra's hits, *The Man with the Golden Arm* (1955) and *A Hole in the Head* (1959).

Parker lived in this Beverly Drive mansion when she co-starred with Frank Sinatra in the 1950s.

Eleanor Parker
620 North Beverly Drive, Beverly Hills

Gregory Peck (1916–2003)
266 South Cliffwood Avenue, Brentwood

Gregory Peck may be most closely identified with the type of character he played in *To Kill a Mockingbird* (1962)—the principled lawyer and father. That performance earned Peck the Best Actor Oscar. Among Peck's other roles were an author who challenges anti-Semitism in *Gentleman's Agreement* (1947), and an over-burdened military officer in *Twelve O'Clock High* (1949).

In the late 1950s, Peck moved from Pacific Palisades to this Brentwood residence. The two-story, red-brick French-provincial house is surrounded by a brick wall and gardens. In 1976 he relocated to Holmby Hills.

Anthony Perkins (1932–1992)
1127 ½ Horn Avenue, West Hollywood

Slender, dark-haired Anthony Perkins may be eternally identified with Norman Bates, the gentle-on-the-outside psychopath he played in the Alfred Hitchcock thriller *Psycho* (1960). Critics also lauded his performances in *Friendly Persuasion* (1956), *Desire Under the Elms* (1958) and *On the Beach* (1959). Perkins revived his Norman Bates character in three *Psycho* sequels.

In the late 1950s, Perkins rented a unit in this small apartment complex located less than a block from Sunset Boulevard. Befitting his screen image, Perkins' former apartment is in the only dark hallway in this otherwise sunny complex.

Jack Pickford (1896–1933)
210 North Serrano Avenue, Los Angeles

Like his famous older sister, Mary Pickford, Jack Pickford got his start in a D.W. Griffith film. In Jack's case the movie was *The Message* (1909). Pickford went on to appear in more than 100 movies. He also directed *Little Lord Fauntleroy* (1921), which starred his sister, Mary.

In 1922, Pickford lived here on a peaceful block near the Wilshire district. His home life as a child was anything but peaceful. After his father died, Pickford's mother worried that she couldn't support her three children, so she sent them each to different foster homes (Jack Pickford was just 2 years old). The Pickford family was eventually reunited.

Mary Pickford (1892–1979)
56 Freemont Place, Los Angeles
426 North Rockingham Avenue, Brentwood

Sixteen-year-old Mary Pickford was already an accomplished stage actress when D.W. Griffith signed her for *Pippa Passes* (1909). It was the first of more than 100 Griffith shorts featuring Pickford, who would go on to become the most famous female movie star of the silent era, and one of the most powerful forces in early Hollywood. Pickford, known as "America's Sweetheart," played plucky girls who found ingenious ways to get out of jams in such hits as *Daddy Long Legs* (1919) and *Pollyanna* (1920).

56 Freemont Place: In 1919, Pickford and her mother rented a large house in this private community in the mid-Wilshire district. She hid out from the press here while waiting for her divorce from her first husband, Owen Moore, to become final. She would then move into Pickfair, the Beverly Hills estate that her second husband, Douglas Fairbanks, built for her. The original Pickfair is no longer standing; a new house was built on the site in 1991. Shortly after entering movies, the penny-wise Pickfair chastised a fellow actress who had just purchased a new hat. "You'll regret anything so silly," she said. "You'll have that worn-out bird of paradise hat. And I'll have property."

426 North Rockingham Avenue: Following their 1937 wedding, Pickford and third husband Buddy Rogers lived in this Brentwood house (which Rogers already owned). Shortly before marrying Rogers, Pickford told a *Liberty Magazine* reporter, "I think—in fact I'm sure—I shall sell Pickfair. For one thing, I want to get a small house on Lake Arrowhead. The sort of place where you can rough it by yourself." She apparently changed her mind. After moving into Roger's Brentwood home, it was only a matter of weeks before Pickford missed her Beverly Hills digs and the couple moved to the Pickfair estate.

Mary Pickford
426 North Rockingham Avenue, Brentwood

Walter Pidgeon (1897–1984)
230 Strada Corta Road, Bel Air

Walter Pidgeon brought an even-tempered personality to some of Hollywood's most popular films, including *Saratoga* (1937), *How Green Was My Valley* (1941) and *Mrs. Miniver* (1942). Pidgeon and Greer Garson starred together in several more movies, including *Madame Curie* (1943) and *Mrs.*

Parkington (1944). A few years before he retired, Pidgeon played Florenz Zeigfeld in *Funny Girl* (1968).

Pidgeon bought this Bel Air Country English-style house in 1940 and lived here for the rest of his life. When reporters came to Pidgeon's home to conduct interviews, the fastidious Pidgeon would peek out of an upstairs window. If a reporter looked disheveled or poorly dressed, Pidgeon would often cancel the interview.

Brad Pitt (1963–)
1026 Ridgedale Drive, Beverly Hills

Brad Pitt's supporting role as the hitchhiking robber in *Thelma and Louise* (1991) marks the first time many moviegoers took notice of the slender young man who would become a major Hollywood heartthrob. Pitt's other notable movies include *A River Runs Through It* (1992), *Seven Years in Tibet* (1997), *Fight Club* (1999) and *Oceans Eleven* (2001).

Pitt and his wife, actress Jennifer Aniston, live on this estate originally built by actor Fredric March. Pitt indulged his love of architecture and interior design by being heavily involved in the home's two-year renovation process. The couple settled into their new home in July 2003.

ZaSu Pitts (1898–1963)
241 North Rockingham Avenue, Brentwood

ZaSu Pitts was a dramatic actress in silent pictures, but when the talkies arrived the studios realized that her high-strung manner and distinctive voice had comic potential. In the early 1930s, Pitts was teamed with Slim Summerville, then with Thelma Todd. In later years she co-starred in

Life with Father (1947) Pitts' first name was formed by combining the names of two aunts, Eliza and Susan.

Architect Paul R. Williams—often called the "Architect to the Stars"—designed the house behind these white gates for Pitts. She moved in during the mid-1930s. Rockingham might be considered Brentwood's walk of fame. Among other former Rockingham residents who, like Pitts, started their movie careers as youngsters: Mary Pickford, Judy Garland and Shirley Temple.

Sidney Poitier (1927–)
1007 Cove Way, Beverly Hills

Sidney Poitier broke the color barrier in 1950's and 1960's Hollywood by taking on parts that veered far from the traditional roles played by black actors at the

time. Poitier became the first black man to be nominated for a Best Actor Oscar for his performance opposite Tony Curtis in *The Defiant Ones* (1958). He went on to win the award—again a first for a black actor—for *Lilies of the Field* (1963).

Poitier lived in this Beverly Hills house for at least a decade before selling it in the mid-1990s. When Poitier came to Hollywood to film *Porgy and Bess* (1959), he lived at the Chateau Marmont (8221 West Sunset Boulevard—see Beatrice Lillie).

Dick Powell (1904–1963)
711 North Maple Drive, Beverly Hills

Early in his career, Warner Brothers leveraged Dick Powell's singing talents by casting him in such musicals as *42nd Street* (1933) and *Footlight Parade* (1933). Powell eventually moved on to more sophisticated fare, such as the Preston Sturgis comedy *Christmas in July* (1940). Around the time he

made one of his last movies, *The Bad and the Beautiful* (1952), Powell began shifting his focus to producing and hosting his own television shows.

Powell and his first wife, actress Joan Blondell, moved to this Beverly Hills house in 1937. The following year they moved to a house near West Hollywood. Powell was a successful real estate investor who eventually owned property throughout Southern California.

William Powell (1892–1984)
809 North Hillcrest Road, Beverly Hills

After playing unscrupulous characters in silent films, William Powell's image was transformed during the 1930s into that of a sophisticated master of droll dialogue. Powell is best known for teaming with Myrna Loy in *The Thin Man* series (1934–1947). Powell also co-starred with Carole Lombard (to whom he was briefly married) in the popular screwball comedy *My Man Godfrey* (1936).

Powell remodeled the house on this estate in the mid-1930s. He once joked that the new architectural style would be "a combination of Regency, Beverly Hills Gothic and early Chester A. Arthur."

Tyrone Power (1913–1958)
139 North Saltair Avenue, Brentwood

Tyrone Power's star began to rise in the late 1930s, when he appeared in *In Old Chicago* (1937) and *Alexander's Ragtime Band* (1938). The dark-eyed leading man went on to be featured in dozens of movies, showing a flair for adventure fare in *The Mark of Zorro* (1940) and *The Black Swan* (1942). He died at 42 from a heart attack.

Power's Georgian-style house was designed by famed Los Angeles architect Paul R. Williams. Power bought the house in the late 1930s. Gary Cooper lived down the street, in a home that is no longer standing.

Elvis Presley (1935–1977)
1174 North Hillcrest Road, Beverly Hills

Elvis Presley was already "The King" of rock 'n' roll when he landed in his first movie, *Love Me Tender* (1956). He went on to star in movies that were heavier on music than story lines, including *G.I. Blues* (1960) and *Blue Hawaii* (1961).

Presley took up residence here in November 1967 and stayed for about three years. He moved to a more private house (which had once belonged to Julie Andrews), after one too many nights of returning home to find fans crowding around the front lawn of this house.

Robert Preston (1918–1987)
436 North Bristol Avenue, Brentwood

Robert Preston played supporting roles in 1930's dramas, then took a detour to the Broadway stage. An expert musician who could play several instruments, Preston earned a Tony Award for his portrayal of Prof. Henry Hills in the Broadway blockbuster *The Music Man*. He returned to Hollywood to reprise that role in the film version of *The Music Man*

(1962). More hits followed, including *Mame* (1974), *Semi-Tough* (1977) and *Victor/Victoria* (1984).

Preston filmed *The Music Man*, among other movies, during the years he lived in this house. It's located a few doors from Joan Crawford's infamous "Mommie Dearest" house (426 North Bristol Avenue—see Joan Crawford).

Vincent Price (1911–1993)
1815 Benedict Canyon Drive, Los Angeles

Vincent Price gained fame as a polished villain, starring in movies such as *The Fly* (1958), *House on Haunted Hill* (1958) and the British-made *Theater of Blood* (1973). Prior to becoming a horror-film hero, Price played his share of conventional roles in such movies as *Song of Bernadette* (1943) and *Laura* (1944).

Price and his family moved into this Benedict Canyon adobe house in the early 1940s. After World War II he built a house on a 10-acre lot in Malibu.

Edna Purviance (1895–1958)
336 North Beachwood Drive, Los Angeles

Edna Purviance was one of Charlie Chaplin's most reliable supporting players. In fact, she worked exclusively for Chaplin. He first signed Purviance for *A Night Out* (1915). She ultimately appeared in every Chaplin short—often playing the leading lady—and seven Chaplin features, including *The Kid* (1921) and *Monsieur Verdoux* (1947).

Purviance's house was about three miles from the Chaplin Studios at 1416 North La Brea, where Purviance worked throughout the 1920s.

Anthony Quinn (1915–2001)
333 Las Casas Avenue, Pacific Palisades

Anthony Quinn played a series of villains until he signed with Warner Brothers, which cast him as a dancer in *City for Conquest* (1940) and later as a bullfighter in *Blood and Sand* (1941). Quinn, who was a busy actor right up to his death, also had important parts in *The Ox-Bow Incident* (1943), *Viva Zapata!* (1952) and *Lawrence of Arabia* (1962).

Quinn lived in this gated Pacific Palisades house in the 1950s. It has an ocean view.

George Raft (1895–1980)
El Royale Apartments
450 North Rossmore Avenue, Hancock Park

George Raft is best known for portraying dour thugs in movies such as *Scarface* (1932). "I'm kind of a greaseball type and I guess some people like me, so I must be passable," he once said. Raft's 51-year film career included a role in Billy Wilder's 1959 comedy, *Some Like It Hot*, in which Raft parodied his own gangster screen image.

In the late 1930s, Raft lived in a penthouse in the El Royale Apartments near Wilshire Boulevard. Among his unusual furnishings was a floor-model radio with a fold-out bar. Raft later bought homes in Coldwater Canyon and Beverly Hills.

Basil Rathbone (1892–1967)
5254 Los Feliz Boulevard, Los Feliz

For a generation of moviegoers, Basil Rathbone was Sherlock Holmes. Rathbone played Sir Arthur Conan Doyle's brilliant detective in 14 movies and many radio programs, starting with the film *The Hound of the Baskervilles* (1939). Rathbone often played villains in other movies, including *David Copperfield* (1935) and *The Adventures of Robin Hood* (1938).

Rathbone and his wife, Ouida, shared this Los Feliz house with seven dogs. Ouida loved to throw parties, making their home something of a social center for their Hollywood friends in the late 1930s.

Basil Rathbone
5254 Los Feliz Boulevard, Los Feliz

Martha Raye (1916–1994)
1153 Roscomare Road, Bel Air

Martha Raye's booming voice was her stock-in-trade. Discovered while singing at The Trocadero Club in Hollywood, Raye was first cast as a supporting player in Bing Crosby's *Rhythm on the Range* (1936). She went on to appear in light fare, including *Double or Nothing* (1937), *Four Jills and a Jeep* (1944) and *Monsieur Verdoux* (1947) in which she played a wife who inspired murderous impulses in Charlie Chaplin.

After Raye bought this house in the early 1960s, Jimmy Durante, who co-starred with her in *Billy Rose's Jumbo* (1962), gave her a house-warming gift. It was a life-sized Santa Claus that danced the twist.

Ronald Reagan (1911–)
1258 Amalfi Drive, Pacific Palisades

Long before he was elected President of the United States, Ronald Reagan appeared in scores of B movies. Occasionally Reagan landed substantial parts in audience favorites, including *Brother Rat* (1940), *Knute Rockne—All-American* (1940) and *Kings Row* (1942). Reagan sharpened his political skills while serving as president of the Screen Actor's Guild from 1947–1952 and 1959–1960.

Reagan and his second wife, Nancy, moved into this ranch-style Pacific Palisades house in 1957. The house, which boasts an expansive view of the Pacific Ocean, continued to be their Los Angeles home base until Reagan was sworn in as President of the United States in 1981.

Donna Reed (1921–1986)
1188 Coldwater Canyon Drive, Beverly Hills

Donna Reed's most renowned movie role was that of James Stewart's supportive wife in *It's a Wonderful Life* (1946). But her most honored role came seven years later when she played a prostitute in *From Here to Eternity* (1953). That performance earned Reed the Academy Award for Best Actress in a Supporting Role. Reed's popularity skyrocketed when she starred in *The Donna Reed Show* (1958–1966) on TV.

Reed's Greek Revival-style house—where she lived while making *The Donna Reed Show*—is reminiscent of a plantation home. It's on Coldwater Canyon Boulevard, a street that is heavily traversed by commuters traveling between the San Fernando Valley and the Beverly Hills area.

George Reeves (1914–1959)
340 North Oakhurst Drive, Beverly Hills

George Reeves' first credited movie appearance was in *Gone With the Wind* (1939). He played Stuart Tarleton, one of the twins smitten with Scarlett O'Hara in the movie's early scenes. After serving in World War II, Reeves returned to Hollywood and found few good opportunities until he was cast as Clark Kent, a.k.a. Superman, in *Superman and the Mole Men* (1951). He went on to star in more Superman movies as well as the TV series, *Adventures of Superman* (1952–1957)

Reeves lived in this Oakhurst Drive apartment building when his career started to gain steam in the early 1940s. In 1959 Reeves was found dead of a gunshot wound at his Benedict Canyon house. There continues to be controversy about whether he committed suicide or was murdered.

Donna Reed
1188 Coldwater Canyon Drive, Beverly Hills

Burt Reynolds (1936–)
245 North Carolwood Drive, Holmby Hills

Like many actors of his era, Burt Reynolds divided his time between TV and movies for several years. He turned his full attention to movies after receiving rave reviews for his performance in *Deliverance* (1972). Reynolds went on to star in such movies as *Smokey and the Bandit* (1977), *Starting Over* (1979) and *Boogie Nights* (1997).

Reynolds, a tabloid favorite during the 1980s, foiled at least one photographer who was waiting for him one day outside of this house. "I managed to bump him hard enough to ruin the film. I was lucky that's all I ruined," Reynolds later recalled in his memoir. When Reynolds put his house up for sale in 1989, it had a bar that ran the full length of his 45-foot long swimming pool. The house belonged previously to Beatle George Harrison.

Debbie Reynolds (1932–)
324 Conway Avenue, Westwood

Debbie Reynolds was in demand during the 1950s and 1960s for girl-next-door parts, especially if the girl had to sing and dance. She co-starred in *Singin' in the Rain* (1952), then starred in such hits as *The Tender Trap* (1955), *How the West Was Won* (1962) and *The Unsinkable Molly Brown* (1964). She later devoted much of her time to the stage, returning for the occasional movie, such as the title role in the Albert Brooks comedy *Mother* (1996).

When she found out that she was pregnant with her second child in 1957, Reynolds decided that her Beverly Hills house was too small. She, husband Eddie Fisher and daughter Carrie moved into this four-bedroom house in Westwood.

Debbie Reynolds
324 Conway Avenue, Westwood

Joe Roberts (1871–1923)
1322 Tamarind Avenue, Hollywood

At 6' 3" and weighing in at nearly 300 pounds, "Big Joe" Roberts made the perfect nemesis for the diminutive Buster Keaton. Although Roberts made occasional forays outside the Keaton studio, he spent most of his career with Keaton, playing supporting roles in 18 Keaton movies.

During the early 1920s, Roberts had to travel less than a mile from this black-trimmed white house to the Buster Keaton Studio.

Edward G. Robinson (1893–1973)
910 Rexford Drive, Beverly Hills

Edward G. Robinson's image as the ruthless, cigar-smoking gangster was established with *Little Caesar* (1930). Robinson also ventured into other genres. He starred in the controversial *Dr. Ehrlich's Magic Bullet* (1940) about a doctor who discovers a cure for syphilis, and later played Fred MacMurray's boss in the film noir classic *Double Indemnity* (1944).

Robinson's Beverly Hills house was lined with original paintings by Impressionist and Post-Impressionist artists. In the mid-1950s, nearly broke after being shunned by the studios for loaning money to blacklisted screenwriter Dalton Trumbo, Robinson had to sell his treasured art collection.

Charles "Buddy" Rogers (1904–1999)
426 Rockingham Avenue, Brentwood

Buddy Rogers played freshly scrubbed young men in movies such as *Wings* (1927), and *My Best Girl* (1927). He starred in the latter with his future wife, Mary Pickford. Rogers wasn't impressed with his own talents. "I was never any good. I couldn't act worth beans," he once said.

Rogers lived here before he married Mary Pickford in 1937. After they married, the couple briefly settled here and made plans to build their own home. Rogers once told a reporter that their new house would not be as "pretentious as Pickfair [Mary Pickford's estate]. Mercy no; only four master bedrooms, and of course tennis courts, swimming pool and things like that."

Ginger Rogers (1911–1995)
1605 Gilcrest Drive, Los Angeles

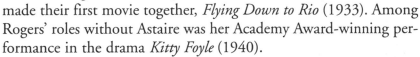

Ginger Rogers and Fred Astaire danced and bantered their way through some of Hollywood's best-loved musicals. Rogers was a Hollywood veteran when they made their first movie together, *Flying Down to Rio* (1933). Among Rogers' roles without Astaire was her Academy Award-winning performance in the drama *Kitty Foyle* (1940).

In 1937, Rogers built this house which is perched on a Coldwater Canyon hilltop that is high enough to offer a coastline view. She frequently entertained on the patio. Rogers' first Hollywood home was the infamous Garden of Allah apartments on Sunset.

Gilbert Roland (1905–1994)
714 North Alpine Drive, Beverly Hills

Gilbert Roland's film career spanned five decades. In the 1920s and 1930s, he was often cast as the stereotypical "Latin lover" in such movies as *Camille* (1926) opposite Norma Talmadge. Roland played the Cisco Kid in six movies, starting with *The Gay Cavalier* (1946). After his movie debut in 1925, Roland changed his name from Luis Antonio Damaso De

Alonso to Gilbert Roland by combining the names of two of his favorite actors: John Gilbert and Ruth Roland.

During the 1930s and 1940s, Roland lived in this comfortable Colonial Revival-style house in Beverly Hills.

Ruth Roland (1892–1937)
1466 North Sweetzer Avenue, West Hollywood

Ruth Roland began appearing in one- and two-reel Westerns while she was a student at Hollywood High School. In fact, she was the first student from that fabled high school to become a movie star. A few years after her film debut, she signed with Mack Sennett, who starred her in *The Girl Detective Series* (1915). Roland went on to star in several serials, including *The Adventures of Ruth* (1919), which she produced herself.

Roland lived here during the 1920s. Today the house is white with green-edged-windows. She became a successful real estate investor

after she left the movies. She once commented that she earned more money while selling Los Angeles real estate for four years than she did while starring in movies for 16 years.

Mickey Rooney (1920–)
15750 Sutton Street, Encino

Mickey Rooney's movie career began as an engaging child actor in a series of two-reelers under the name "Joe Yule Jr." Changing his name to Mickey Rooney, he continued to play irrepressible youngsters in movies such as *My Pal the King* (1932) with Tom Mix, and *Manhattan Melodrama* (1934) with Clark Gable. But it was Rooney's pairing with Judy Garland for such movies as *The Courtship of Andy Hardy* (1942) and *Girl Crazy* (1943) that made him a star.

In the fall of 1938, 18-year-old Rooney paid $75,000 for this house in Encino. At the time it was on a five-acre parcel of land. Rooney moved into the 12-room house with his mother, Nell.

Rosalind Russell (1907–1976)
706 North Beverly Drive, Beverly Hills

Rosalind Russell was often cast as a sharp-tongued career woman in movies such as *His Girl Friday* (1940), in which she verbally sparred with Cary Grant. Her breakout role came the year before in *The Women* (1939). Nearly two decades later she was the fun-loving Mame in *Auntie Mame* (1958).

In 1942, Russell and husband, producer Frederick Brisson, bought this Beverly Hills house from actress Mary Boland, one of Russell's co-stars in *The Women*. Russell took care of much of the gardening herself. A jade tree near one of the living room windows was a gift from Barbara Hutton, the Woolworth heiress and wife of Cary Grant.

Ann Rutherford (1920–)
826 Greenway Drive, Beverly Hills

Ann Rutherford is well known to *Andy Hardy* fans as Polly Benedict, the often-perturbed girlfriend of Andy, played by Mickey Rooney. In addition to appearing in 12 of the 16 *Andy Hardy* movies between 1938 and 1942, Rutherford landed a role in one of the biggest blockbusters of them all—she played Scarlett O'Hara's sister, Carreen, in *Gone With the Wind* (1939). Rutherford also co-starred in *Pride and Prejudice* (1940) and *The Secret Life of Walter Mitty* (1947).

Rutherford has lived in this Georgian-style house for at least 30 years. A close observer of the Beverly Hills social scene over the years, Rutherford told a writer in 1976, "There was a time from perhaps 1936 to 1966, when if you gave a party worthy of being called a party, it had to be under a tent. After you sent your invitations and reminders up front, you met with your caterer and tent man to plan everything. Those are very few and far between now, and I think it's a blessing."

Eva Marie Saint (1924–)
900 North Stone Canyon Road, Bel Air

Eva Marie Saint's moving performance opposite Marlon Brando in *On the Waterfront* (1954) earned her the Academy Award for Best Supporting Actress in her very first screen role. She soon turned her attention to TV, but returned to the screen for a handful of important movies, including *North by Northwest* (1959), *Exodus* (1960) and *The Sandpiper* (1965).

This is where Saint lived during the era when she made such classics as *North by Northwest.* Her house near the Hotel Bel Air is in the heart of Bel Air Estates, a region that was established in the late 1900s by developer Alphonzo Bell.

Roy Scheider (1932–)
Sunset Marquis Hotel and Villas
1200 Alta Loma Road, West Hollywood

Roy Scheider faced down sharks as Police Chief Martin Brody in *Jaws* (1975) and *Jaws 2* (1978), and then death as choreographer Joe Gideon in *All That Jazz* (1979). The latter performance earned Scheider his second Oscar nomination. His first nomination was for his supporting role in *The French Connection* (1971). Scheider wound up in *Jaws 2* because he abruptly quit *The Deer Hunter* (1978). Universal would let Scheider leave the production only if he agreed to appear in *Jaws 2*. His *Deer Hunter* part ultimately went to Robert De Niro.

Scheider stayed at the Sunset Marquis Hotel and Villas in the 1970s and 1980s while filming movies in Los Angeles. He usually stayed in a guesthouse that has since been converted to the hotel's concierge office.

Eva Marie Saint
900 North Stone Canyon Road, Bel Air

Joseph Schildkraut (1896–1964)
812 North Roxbury Drive, Beverly Hills

Austrian native Joseph Schildkraut made his U.S. film debut as Lillian Gish's love interest in *Orphans of the Storm* (1922). In 1937 Schildkraut was awarded the Oscar for Best Supporting Actor for his portrayal of Captain Dreyfuss in *The Life of Emile Zola* (1937). One of his final performances was as Otto Frank in *The Diary of Anne Frank* (1959), a role he originated on Broadway.

Schildkraut resided in this four-bedroom Tudor-inspired house in the 1950s. He decided to move to California from Austria in the mid-1920s after Cecil B. DeMille signed him and his father, actor Rudolph Schildkraut, to five-year contracts. "When we first came to Hollywood, it looked to us more like a spot in the South of France than an American town," he wrote many years later.

Arnold Schwarzenegger (1947–)
14209 Sunset Boulevard, Pacific Palisades

Arnold Schwarzenegger was already a world-championship bodybuilder when he played a bodybuilder in *Stay Hungry* (1976). It proved to be a springboard to such action movies as *Conan the Barbarian* (1982) and the *Terminator* movies (1991, 1996 and 2003) for which Schwarzenegger has become known. He took a break from his movie career to be elected governor of California in 2003.

This private street leads to the five-acre compound where Schwarzenegger and his family lived from the mid-1980s until 2002. The property includes three houses, three swimming pools and three tennis courts.

George C. Scott (1927–1999)
156 Copley Place, Beverly Hills

George C. Scott, an actor with a jagged voice and forceful manner, starred in films like *The List of Adrian Messenger* (1963), *Dr. Strangelove* (1964), *Patton* (1970) and *The Hospital* (1971). Scott won the Academy Award for Best Actor for *Patton*, but he declined to accept the award. He called the ceremony "a two-hour meat parade."

A stand of palm trees adorns the front of Scott's house, located at the end of a cul-de-sac. He owned this house in the 1980s. He and his wife, actress Trish Van Devere, divided their time between Beverly Hills and Greenwich, Connecticut.

Randolph Scott (1898–1987)
2177 West Live Oak Drive, Hollywood Hills

Such Westerns as *The Last of the Mohicans* (1936) and *The Spoilers* (1942) were Randolph Scott's specialty for many years. His forays outside the Western genre included supporting roles in two Fred Astaire and Ginger Rogers films—*Roberta* (1935) and *Follow The Fleet* (1936)—and the Shirley Temple movie *Rebecca of Sunnybrook Farm* (1938).

Scott roomed with his close friend, Cary Grant, off and on throughout his movie career. In the early 1930s, the two shared this Spanish-style house in the Hollywood Hills.

Norma Shearer (1902–1983)
707 Palisades Beach Road, Santa Monica

Norma Shearer played two important roles in MGM history: She co-starred in the studio's first film, *He Who Gets Slapped* (1924), and she married the highly respected MGM production chief, Irving Thalberg. Shearer was featured in some of the most popular dramas of the 1920s and 1930s, including *The Divorcee* (1930), for which she earned a Best Actress Oscar, *Strange Interlude* (1932) and *The Women* (1939).

This Santa Monica beach house, shared by Shearer and Thalberg, has changed little since the couple used it as an escape from the hubbub of Hollywood in the 1930s. Shearer said of the house, "I want it comfortable and homey—something Irving will look forward to at the end of a hard day at the studio." The house was sealed and air conditioned because it was thought that the ocean air could worsen Thalberg's heart problems.

Phil Silvers (1911–1985)
717 North Alpine Drive, Beverly Hills

During the 1940s, Phil Silvers played brash characters in comedies such as *You're in the Army Now* (1941)
and *Cover Girl* (1944). Following award-winning stints
on Broadway and TV, Silvers appeared on the big screen again in *It's
a Mad Mad Mad Mad World* (1963) in which he played the most
money grubbing of the film's treasure hunters.

This was Silvers' home of many years. When he moved from New
York to Los Angeles to tape *The Phil Silvers Show*, he rented a house
in Beverly Hills while shopping for his own home. "A house was very
important to me. I was fifty-years-old and I'd never owned one,"
noted Silvers in his memoir.

Frank Sinatra (1915–1998)
915 North Foothill Road, Beverly Hills

Frank Sinatra had already conquered the record business when he decided to take on Hollywood as well.
He lobbied for, and won, the role of the soldier who
put his life on the line by standing up to the callous sergeant played
by Ernest Borgnine in *From Here To Eternity* (1953). The performance earned Sinatra the Academy Award for Best Supporting Actor.
He proceeded to appear in such movies as *Guys and Dolls* (1955),
The Man with the Golden Arm (1955) and *Von Ryan's Express* (1965).

Sinatra and his fourth wife,
Barbara, moved into this Beverly
Hills estate in the mid-1980s. A
few years later they added a second floor. The 9,000-square-foot
house sports an art gallery and a
gym. It sold for close to $7.9 mil-
lion in 2003.

Phil Silvers
717 North Alpine Drive, Beverly Hills

Elke Sommer (1940–)
540 North Beverly Glen Boulevard
Holmby Hills

Elke Sommer acted in European movies before getting a small role in the American film *The Victors* (1963) with George Hamilton. She also appeared with Paul Newman in *The Prize* (1963) and with Peter Sellers in *A Shot in the Dark* (1964).

Like many Holmby Hills houses, Sommer's long-time home is hidden behind lush vegetation. Today, the 4,095-square-foot house has three bedrooms and four bathrooms.

James Spader (1960–)
9530 Heather Road, Los Angeles

James Spader earned praise from audiences and critics alike for his portrayal of the oddball videographer in *Sex, Lies and Videotape* (1989). Spader also played interesting—if unsavory—characters in movies such as *Wall Street* (1987), *Wolf* (1994) and *Secretary* (2002).

This gray house with white trim is just off of Coldwater Canyon Drive near Beverly Hills. Spader lived here for several years before selling it in late 2003.

James Spader
9530 Heather Road, Los Angeles

Robert Stack (1919–2003)
321 Saint Pierre Road, Bel Air

His take-charge manner made Robert Stack a popular choice for such movies as the World War II drama *Eagle Squadron* (1942), as well as *Bwana Devil* (1952) and *Written on the Wind* (1956). Stack became known to TV audiences when he starred in *The Untouchables* (1959–1963), and later hosted *Unsolved Mysteries*.

Stack's estate, which he bought in the late 1940s, originally belonged to silent star Colleen Moore. In his memoir, Stack recounted how, five years after he moved in, he discovered a room filled with canisters containing Moore's movies, screen tests and home movies. After watching the movies of his home's original owner, Stack said, "I became an instant fan." In 1958, Stack replaced the original house with the mansion that stands today. He lived there for several more decades.

Sylvester Stallone (1946–)
1575 Capri Drive, Pacific Palisades

Sylvester Stallone became a star when he played boxer Rocky Balboa in *Rocky* (1976). The movie, for which Stallone also wrote the screenplay, won the Academy Award for Best Picture. His action movies, such as the *Rambo* series (1982–1990), earned big box-office receipts.

Neighbors didn't like a tall red-brick wall on this estate formerly owned by Stallone. In 1986, they filed a lawsuit against him, charging that the wall violated community ordinances. (This view of the house is from Amalfi Drive.)

Harry Dean Stanton (1926–)
2597 North Beachwood Drive, Hollywood Hills

Harry Dean Stanton's career got a boost after Sam Peckinpah cast him in a supporting role in *Pat Garrett and Billy the Kid* (1973). The weathered-faced actor went on to play outcasts in such movies as *Alien* (1979); *Paris, Texas* (1984); and *The Green Mile* (1999). Stanton is also an accomplished guitarist and singer who frequently performs with his band in Southern California.

While making movies in the 1960s and 1970s, Stanton lived in a rear unit of this Spanish-style complex. It's located in Hollywood Dell, a neighborhood that is in the shadow of the landmark Hollywood sign.

Barbara Stanwyck (1907–1990)
273 South Beverly Glen Boulevard, Westwood

Barbara Stanwyck was among the most popular leading ladies of Hollywood's golden age. She began her film career as a staple of weepy melodramas. By the late 1930s, she had graduated to critically acclaimed box office hits, seducing Henry Fonda in *The Lady Eve* (1941) and plotting the perfect crime in the Billy Wilder noir classic *Double Indemnity* (1944).

This was one of Stanwyck's homes during the 1950s. Years before she moved into this Westwood house, Stanwyck and actor Robert Taylor owned a ranch in Northridge and houses in Beverly Hills and San Marino.

Jan Sterling (1923–2004)
7141 Senalda Road, Hollywood Hills

After a brief Broadway stage career, Jan Sterling came west and won a role in *Johnny Belinda* (1948). She went on to play underhanded women in such movies as *Ace in the Hole* (1951), directed by Billy Wilder, and *Flesh and Fury* (1952) opposite Tony Curtis. Sterling earned an Oscar nomination for her performance in *The High and the Mighty* (1954).

Sterling and her husband, actor Paul Douglas, had a view of the Outpost Estates area of Hollywood. They lived here during the 1950s.

James Stewart (1908–1997)
1262 Coldwater Canyon Drive, Beverly Hills

Whether he played a cowboy or a politician, audiences couldn't get enough of James Stewart's unassuming charm. His long list of revered movies includes *You Can't Take It With You* (1938), *Mr. Smith Goes to Washington* (1939), *The Philadelphia Story* (1940), *The Shop Around the Corner* (1940), *It's a Wonderful Life* (1946) and *Rear Window* (1954). Stewart's performance as the reporter who is smitten with Katharine Hepburn in *The Philadelphia Story* earned him the Oscar for Best Actor in 1940.

After they married, Stewart and his wife, Gloria, moved into this Coldwater Canyon house where Gloria had already been living before the marriage. Stewart's own pre-marriage house was in Brentwood. Hollywood columnist Hedda Hopper described Stewart's bachelor abode: "The house was utterly devoid of ornamentation, was as plain as Jimmy and a great deal more severe. For pin-ups, Jimmy had sketches of airplanes."

James Stewart
1262 Coldwater Canyon Drive, Beverly Hills

Sharon Stone (1958–)
7809 Torreyson Drive, Hollywood Hills

Part sex symbol, part dramatic actress, Sharon Stone's career has included turns as a murder suspect in *Basic Instinct* (1992), a drug addicted wife of a mobster in *Casino* (1995) and a light-hearted muse in *The Muse* (1999).

Stone bought this 1,900-square-foot ranch-style house in 1989, and sold it in the late 1990s. The house, located off of Mulholland Drive, has views of the San Fernando Valley and the mountains.

Barbra Streisand (1942–)
904 North Bedford Drive, Beverly Hills

Barbra Streisand might be considered the consummate entertainer. She's won two Oscars as well as Emmy, Tony and Grammy Awards for her acting, singing and songwriting. She has also served as producer, director and writer for many of her movies. Streisand earned the Academy Award for Best Actress for her debut film, *Funny Girl* (1968). Eight years later she and Paul Williams won the Oscar for Best Song for "Evergreen," from *A Star Is Born* (1976).

In 1967, Streisand arrived in Los Angeles to film *Funny Girl*. She and her year-old son, Jason Gould, moved into this house, which had been occupied by Greta Garbo many years earlier. Around the time she began shooting *On A Clear Day* (1970), Streisand purchased a house in Holmby Hills. In later years Streisand owned a Malibu ranch. In 1994 she tried to sell it. When she couldn't find a buyer who was willing to pay her asking price, she donated the property to the Santa Monica Mountains Conservancy.

Barbra Streisand
904 North Bedford Drive, Beverly Hills

Donald Sutherland (1935–)
548 Crestline Drive, Brentwood

Many of Donald Sutherland's characters have an air of eccentricity about them. In *The Dirty Dozen* (1967), he was among the band of convicts under Lee Marvin's command and in *M*A*S*H* (1970) he played rebel surgeon Hawkeye Pierce. Sutherland also co-starred in *Klute* (1971) and *Ordinary People* (1980). His son is actor Kiefer Sutherland.

During the 1980s, Donald Sutherland lived in this Mediterranean-style Brentwood house, which includes an indoor spa and a detached guesthouse.

Grady Sutton (1906–1995)
1207 North Orange Drive, #207, Hollywood

W. C. Fields used Grady Sutton to his comic advantage by casting him as clueless chumps who Fields easily dupes. Sutton appeared with Fields in *The Pharmacist*

(1933), *The Man on the Flying Trapeze* (1935), *You Can't Cheat an Honest Man* (1941) and *The Bank Dick* (1940). Sutton also played Carole Lombard's dim-witted fiancé in *My Man Godfrey* (1936). He played small roles in movies well into the 1970s.

Sutton lived in this apartment building in the heart of Hollywood around the time he appeared in such movies as *I Love You Alice B. Toklas* (1968) and *Myra Breckenridge* (1970).

Gloria Swanson (1897–1983)
1636 ½ Kingsley Drive, Los Feliz

During her six decades in front of the camera, Gloria Swanson's roles ranged from a slapstick comedienne in the early Mack Sennett comedies, to a has-been movie queen in *Sunset Boulevard* (1950). Many critics consider Swanson's performances in silents such as *Manhandled* (1924) and *Sadie Thompson* (1928) to be the best of her career.

Swanson was on the verge of stardom in 1918 when she rented this unit in the rear of a bungalow court. The court was then known as Court Corrine. Sixty-two years later she recalled in her memoir, "Mother and I moved up in the world from St. Francis Court to Court Corrine, which was a double row of modest bungalows in a good location near the studios. The social life of the place consisted mostly of movie gossip and parties and sunbathing."

Blanche Sweet (1896–1986)
601 North Camden Drive, Beverly Hills

Blanche Sweet was D.W. Griffith's leading actress until she jumped ship when Griffith cast Lillian Gish over her in *The Birth of a Nation* (1915). The blonde-bobbed Sweet went on to star in several Cecil B. DeMille productions, including *The Warrens of Virginia* (1915).

Sweet shared this house on a corner lot with her husband, director Marshall Neilan, in the mid-1920s.

Norma Talmadge (1897–1957)
1336 North Harper Avenue, West Hollywood
1038 Palisades Beach Road, Santa Monica

Norma Talmadge was one of the most admired dramatic actresses of the silent era. Shortly after she married producer Joseph M. Schenck in 1916, the couple started their own production company. Among her notable films were *Smilin' Through* (1922), *Kiki* (1926) and *Camille* (1926). Talmadge appeared in two talkies but her voice didn't take well to sound. Before retiring, she performed on the radio with her second husband, George Jessell.

1336 North Harper Avenue: Talmadge had an apartment in this elaborate Mission-style building in Los Angeles' mid-Wilshire district in the early 1930s.

1038 Palisades Beach Road: Talmadge's beachfront, Norman-style home was designed by architect Paul Roe Crawley. In the mid-1930s, she sold this house to Cary Grant and Randolph Scott. In the late 1940s, actor Brian Aherne bought the house and rented it to such high-profile tenants as Howard Hughes, Irving Berlin and Grace Kelly (after she became the Princess of Monaco).

Norma Talmadge
1336 North Harper Avenue, West Hollywood

Akim Tamiroff (1899–1972)
629 North Alta Drive, Beverly Hills

Akim Tamiroff was touring the United States with a Russian acting troupe in 1923 when he scored parts on the New York stage. By the mid-1930s, Hollywood was casting Tamiroff in roles that called for bad guys with a conscience. He played key roles in *Union Pacific* (1939), *The Great McGinty* (1940) and *Touch of Evil* (1958).

In the 1940s, Tamiroff lived in this brick, Tudor-style house on the west end of Beverly Hills.

Elizabeth Taylor (1932–)
700 Nimes Road, Bel Air

Elizabeth Taylor's beauty and glamorous life often overshadowed her acting efforts. Taylor's many box office hits include *National Velvet* (1945), *Father of the*

Bride (1950), *A Place in the Sun* (1951), *Giant* (1956) and *Who's Afraid of Virginia Woolf* (1966). Along the way, Taylor's eventful love life and a series of health problems have made her a Hollywood gossip columnist's dream.

After separating from Senator John Warner in 1981, Taylor bought this former estate of Frank Sinatra's first wife, Nancy. She filled it with English antiques and paintings by Renoir, Van Gogh, and other French Impressionists and Post-Impressionists.

Akim Tamiroff
629 North Alta Drive, Beverly Hills

Robert Taylor (1911–1969)
1709 San Remo Drive, Pacific Palisades

Robert Taylor's first big hit was the original version of *Magnificent Obsession* (1935), co-starring Irene Dunne. He went on to star opposite other leading ladies of the day, including Barbara Stanwyck (who he later married) in *His Brother's Wife* (1936), and Greta Garbo in *Camille* (1937). Taylor's reputation among some of his peers was tarnished in the 1950s when he gave several names to the House Un-American Activities Committee that was investigating Communist sympathizers in Hollywood.

Taylor moved to this Pacific Palisades residence with his wife and new son in 1955. Four years later he bought a 113-acre ranch in Mandeville Canyon, across the street from Dick Powell and June Allyson's 68-acre estate (3100 Mandeville Canyon Road—see June Allyson).

Rod Taylor (1929–)
2375 Bowmont Drive, Los Angeles

Rod Taylor arrived in Hollywood from Australia to appear in *The Virgin Queen* (1955) with Bette Davis. He went on to co-star in *Giant* (1956), *The Birds* (1963) and *A Gathering of Eagles* (1963) among other hits, before turning to action-adventure fare such as *The Deadly Trackers* (1973).

Taylor's Coldwater Canyon home is a far cry from his accommodations as a Hollywood newcomer in 1954. In those days he lived in a tiny room near the beach in Malibu.

Robert Taylor
1709 San Remo Drive, Pacific Palisades

Shirley Temple (1928–)
948 24th Street, Santa Monica
209 North Rockingham Avenue, Brentwood

By the time Shirley Temple was 10 years old, she had been the world's highest-paid movie star thanks to such hits as *Bright Eyes* (1934), *Curly Top* (1935) and *Rebecca of Sunnybrook Farm* (1938). The most famous child actor ever, Temple's popularity also spawned a cottage industry, which turned out Shirley Temple dolls and other toys. Temple continued acting until she was 20. In 1969, she was appointed U.S. representative to the United Nations. She later served as U.S. ambassador to Ghana and Czechoslovakia, and was the first woman to serve as White House Chief of Protocol.

948 24th Street: As a young child, Temple lived in this Santa Monica house with her family.

209 North Rockingham Avenue: The Temple family moved to this Brentwood home shortly after Temple became a major star. Behind the house stood a cottage that Shirley made her own with a soda fountain and her huge doll collection. The cottage also had a maid's quarters and a bomb shelter.

Shirley Temple
948 24th Street, Santa Monica

Thelma Todd (1905–1935)
17575 Pacific Coast Highway
Pacific Palisades

Thelma Todd can be seen in comedies starring Laurel & Hardy, Charley Chase and the Marx Brothers. She also made 17 short comedies with ZaSu Pitts in the early 1930s. Todd's death at the age of 30 shocked Hollywood. Mobster Lucky Luciano was blamed by many for her death, which was caused by carbon monoxide poisoning from her car.

In 1934, Todd opened a restaurant called Thelma Todd's Sidewalk Café in this building. She moved into an apartment above the restaurant. A year later Todd was found dead in a garage located two streets behind the restaurant.

Spencer Tracy (1900–1967)
9191 Saint Ives Drive, Hollywood Hills

Spencer Tracy was one of the most revered actors of his day. Among his early hits were the screwball comedy *Libeled Lady* (1936), co-starring Jean Harlow and William Powell, and his favorite role, that of the high-spirited fisherman Manuel in *Captains Courageous* (1937). Tracy earned an Academy Award for Best Actor for that performance, as he did for his portrayal of Father Flanagan in *Boys Town* (1938). He later teamed with his off-screen lover, Katharine Hepburn, for several comedies as well as his final film, *Guess Who's Coming to Dinner* (1967).

In addition to his home of many years on St. Ives Drive, Tracy owned a 12-acre ranch in Encino. In the early 1940s he moved into the Beverly Hills Hotel's room 491, a top floor corner suite.

Thelma Todd
17575 Pacific Coast Highway, Pacific Palisades

Lana Turner (1921–1995)
730 North Bedford Drive, Beverly Hills

Lana Turner—famously discovered at a drugstore across the street from Hollywood High School—personified 1950's filmland glamour. *The Postman Always Rings Twice* (1947), *Peyton Place* (1957) and *Imitation of Life* (1959) were among her most popular films. In 1958, Turner's personal life made headlines when her daughter, Cheryl, fatally stabbed Turner's mobster boyfriend, Johnny Stompanato.

Turner's boyfriend was killed in her bedroom, just three days after Turner and her daughter moved into this Beverly Hills house. The house had been built by Laura Hope Crews who played Aunt Pittypat in *Gone With the Wind* (1939).

Ben Turpin (1869–1940)
602 North Canon Drive, Beverly Hills

The cross-eyed, slapstick comic Ben Turpin played supporting roles in dozens of Essany comedies before joining the Mack Sennett Studios in 1917. At Sennett, he made movies that lampooned the popular dramas of the day. One of these hits was *The Shriek of Araby* (1923), which made fun of Rudolph Valentino's *The Sheik* (1921).

Turpin lived in this Spanish-style bungalow in the mid-1920s. Turpin invested heavily in real estate. The frugal actor was known to personally handle some of the upkeep at apartment buildings he owned.

Helen Twelvetrees (1908–1958)
6851 Iris Circle, Hollywood Hills

Helen Twelvetrees, a petite blonde with a memorable name, appeared in a number of 1930's melodramas such as *The Painted Desert* (1931) with Clark Gable and William Boyd, and *State's Attorney* (1932) opposite John Barrymore. In 1939, she left Hollywood for a stage career.

Twelvetrees lived in this sprawling house in the early 1930s. It's located on a circular one-way street in the Hollywood Hills, and today overlooks the 101 freeway.

Rudolph Valentino (1895–1926)
692 Valencia Street, Los Angeles
1436 Bella Drive, Los Angeles

Rudolph Valentino, with his slicked-back hair and penetrating stare, may have been Hollywood's first male sex symbol. A series of costume dramas fueled Valentino's fame. He played a war hero in *The Four Horsemen of the Apocalypse* (1921), an Arabian sheik in *The Sheik* (1921) and a matador in *Blood and Sand* (1922). Following his sudden death from peritonitis at the age of 31, thousands of fans attended his funeral in New York. Tens of thousands more lined railroad tracks to pay their respects as his casket was transported to Hollywood for burial.

692 Valencia Street: Valentino was one year away from superstardom in 1920 when he lived in this Valencia Street building in downtown Los Angeles.

1436 Bella Drive: In 1925, Valentino bought this estate, and dubbed it "The Falcon Lair." It is located within two miles of Beverly Hills. He named it after *The Hooded Falcon*, an aborted movie project for which his wife, Natasha Rambova, had written the screenplay. A stable on the estate housed the Arabian horses that Valentino

took out for his early morning horseback rides through the hills surrounding his estate.

Lee Van Cleef (1925–1989)
19471 Rosita Street, Tarzana

Lee Van Cleef's first movie role set the tone for his career. He played an outlaw in the classic Western *High Noon* (1952). Van Cleef, who once said, "Being born with a pair of beady eyes is the best thing that ever happened to me," continued to play hard-boiled characters in movies such as *How the*

West Was Won (1962), and "spaghetti Westerns" such as *For a Few Dollars More* (1967) and *The Good, The Bad, and The Ugly* (1967).

In addition to the San Fernando Valley house at the end of this driveway, Van Cleef and his wife, Barbara, owned a waterfront house in the Channel Islands Marina.

Conrad Veidt (1893–1943)
720 North Foothill Road, Beverly Hills

Conrad Veidt's career began in Germany where he played his most famous role, the sinister Cesare in *The Cabinet of Dr. Caligari* (1919). He came to Hollywood in 1926 at the urging of John Barrymore. Veidt returned to Europe a few years later, but came back in 1940. Veidt continued to be cast as forbidding characters such as the Grand Vizier in *The Thief of Bagdad* (1940) and Major Strasser in *Casablanca* (1942).

Veidt lived on Foothill during his first stay in California. His Spanish Colonial Revival house was built in 1924 for actress Ruth Clifford.

Lupe Velez (1908–1944)
1826 Laurel Canyon Boulevard, Hollywood Hills

Lupe Velez set herself apart from other character actresses by incorporating her nervous energy and prominent Mexican accent into her screen persona. After co-starring with Douglas Fairbanks in *The Goucho* (1927), Velez co-starred with Gary Cooper in *Lady of the Pavements* (1929) and *Wolf Song* (1929). Her later movies included a series of comedies called *Mexican Spitfire* (1940–1943).

Velez lived with Gary Cooper in this Laurel Canyon house for a few years in the early 1930s. Cooper's parents didn't approve of Velez, so she and Cooper soon parted company.

Robert Wagner (1930–)
3331 Laurel Canyon Boulevard, Studio City

Robert Wagner's roles have ranged from a murderous college student in *A Kiss Before Dying* (1956), to a funny character named "Number Two" in the *Austin Powers* movies (1997, 1999, 2002). In between, he's had supporting roles in such movies as *The Longest Day* (1962) and *Harper* (1966). Wagner, who was married to Natalie Wood twice, also starred in the hit TV series *To Catch a Thief* (1968–1970) and *Hart to Hart* (1979–1984).

Wagner lived here during the 1950s. He has also owned a house in Bel Air and horse ranches near Thousand Oaks and in Northern California.

Denzel Washington (1954–)
4701 Sancola Avenue, North Hollywood

After generating a following as Dr. Phillip Chandler on the TV show *St. Elsewhere* (1982–1988), Denzel Washington played the anti-apartheid crusader Steve Biko in *Cry Freedom* (1987). He followed that with other hits, including *Glory* (1989), *Malcolm X* (1992) and *Philadelphia* (1993). In 2002 Washington won the Best Actor Oscar for his performance as a corrupt cop in *Training Day* (2001).

In the late 1980s, Washington lived in this Georgian-style North Hollywood house where actor William Holden had lived in the 1950s.

Denzel Washington
4701 Sancola Avenue, North Hollywood

❖

John Wayne (1907–1979)
207 West Windsor Road, Glendale
6141 Afton Place, Hollywood

Few personify old Hollywood's idea of the all-American man like John Wayne. Wayne became a star with *Stagecoach* (1939), which was directed by his friend, John Ford. He continued to portray the proverbial tough-but-tender man in movies such as *They Were Expendable* (1945), *She Wore a Yellow Ribbon* (1949) and the movie for which he won the Academy Award for Best Actor, *True Grit* (1969). Wayne, who carefully guarded his image, once refused a director's request that he shoot a man in the back in a movie scene.

207 West Windsor Road: Wayne grew up in the Los Angeles suburbs of Lancaster and Glendale. During Wayne's teenage years, he lived with his family in this Glendale apartment building.

6141 Afton Place: Five years after making his first screen appearance, Wayne moved into this Hollywood apartment building, which today is a National Historical Landmark. He made his home in the San Fernando Valley in the 1950s. In 1963 he moved south to Newport Beach, California. Wayne's homes were filled with antiques. Contrary to his tough-guy image, Wayne liked nothing better than poking around antique shops when shooting movies on location.

John Wayne
6141 Afton Place, Hollywood

Johnny Weissmuller (1904–1984)
2 Latimer Road, Santa Monica

After swimmer Johnny Weissmuller earned a total of five gold medals in the 1924 and 1928 Olympics, MGM asked him to play Tarzan. His first Tarzan movie was *Tarzan the Ape Man* (1932) and he repeated the role 11 more times. Weissmuller continued to play jungle- and animal-friendly characters through the 1950s.

In 1943, Weissmuller's wife insisted that the family move from a Brentwood mansion to this smaller house in Santa Monica because she couldn't find enough domestic help to care for the mansion. Weissmuller wasn't happy with the move, in part because this house didn't have a pool. He had been getting back into shape with workouts that included a daily swim.

Orson Welles (1915–1985)
8545 Franklin Avenue, Hollywood Hills

Orson Welles hit the jackpot with his second film, *Citizen Kane* (1941), an epic loosely based on the life of William Randolph Hearst. In addition to playing the lead and co-writing the screenplay, Wells also directed and produced the picture. Wells followed that triumph with such movies as *The Magnificent Ambersons* (1942), *The Third Man* (1950) and *Touch of Evil* (1958).

Orson Welles lived in Brentwood while he wrapped up *Citizen Kane*, but by the time the movie was released, he had scaled back his living

quarters. He rented this Cape Cod-style house in the Hollywood Hills. The house was owned by Sidney Tolar—who played Charlie Chan in the popular Charlie Chan film series.

Johnny Weissmuller
2 Latimer Road, Santa Monica

Mae West (1892–1980)
Ravenswood Apartments
570 North Rossmore Avenue, Hancock Park

Mae West first sashayed onto the screen in 1932, when she appeared opposite George Raft in *Night After Night*. Although she made only 12 movies (serving as a writer as well as star of many), West's outsized persona and double entendres have made her one of Hollywood's most recognizable personalities.

West moved into apartment number 611 in the Ravenswood Apartments in 1932 and stayed for 48 years. Several other stars, including Clark Gable, have also lived at the Ravenswood. West decorated her two-bedroom unit with French provincial furnishings and a lot of mirrors. For security, she installed bulletproof glass windows and a reinforced steel door. Always looking for ways to stay youthful, West kept her blinds drawn and her windows closed to protect her skin from sunlight and fresh air.

Richard Widmark (1914–)
1727 Mandeville Canyon Road, Brentwood

Richard Widmark established himself early in his career as an actor capable of startling audiences with a quick and often cruel temper. *Night and the City* (1950), *The Alamo*, (1960), *Judgment at Nuremberg* (1961) and *How the West Was Won* (1962) were among his most important movies.

In addition to this Mandeville Canyon estate, Widmark has spent much of his time at his 80-acre ranch in the Hidden Valley area of the San Fernando Valley.

Mae West
Ravenswood Apartments, 570 North Rossmore Avenue, Hancock Park

Esther Williams (1922–)
2077 Mandeville Canyon Road, Brentwood

University of Southern California swimming star Esther Williams was set to compete in the 1940 Olympics, but they were cancelled due to the war raging in Europe. Williams instead displayed her swimming talents on the big screen. She gave elaborately choreographed aquatic performances in movies such as *Neptune's Daughter* (1949), in which she introduced the song "Baby, It's Cold Outside."

Williams and her family moved to this Mandeville Canyon property in 1952. They spent $100,000 to turn a cabin into a five-bedroom house. The one-acre property boasts a 400-year-old oak tree, the oldest tree in the canyon. Williams later moved to Bel Air and then Beverly Hills.

Shelley Winters (1922–)
457 North Oakhurst Drive, Beverly Hills

With a decade of supporting parts under her belt, Shelley Winters landed the pivotal role of the frustrated factory worker in *A Place in the Sun* (1951). She went on to win Academy Awards for Best Supporting Actress for her performances in *The Diary of Anne Frank* (1959) and *A Patch of Blue* (1965).

Winters and her husband, actor Vittorio Gassman, purchased this Beverly Hills duplex apartment house in the early 1950s. Gassman hoped that Winters' parents would live in one of the units but they declined the offer. In her memoir, Winters described the location as being "on the wrong side of the railroad tracks from where the superstars lived."

Natalie Wood (1938–1981)
9060 Harland Avenue, West Hollywood

Thanks to her persevering stage mother, Natalie Wood's career was established early. After landing an important role in what was to become a holiday classic, *Miracle on 34th Street* (1947), Wood proceeded to co-star in such films as *Rebel Without a Cause* (1955), *West Side Story* (1961) and *Splendor in the Grass* (1961).

Wood was still known by her real name, Natasha Gurdin, when she and her family settled into this West Hollywood bungalow in 1945. The family moved to the San Fernando Valley during Natalie's high school years. In the mid-1950s they relocated to a house in Laurel Canyon where Wood decorated her bedroom in a modern black and white motif.

James Woods (1947–)
1612 Gilcrest Drive, Los Angeles

Known for bringing intelligence and intensity to his roles, James Woods earned fame early in his film career for portraying misfits in such movies as *The Onion Field*

(1979) and *Best Seller* (1987). In recent years he has played more benign characters in movies that include *Any Given Sunday* (1999) and *The Virgin Suicides* (2000).

Woods owned this house from the early 1980s to the mid-1990s. The house, which is built close to the curb, is one of two properties he owned on Gilcrest Drive. Across the street is the estate where actress Ginger Rogers lived for decades (1605 Gilcrest Drive— see Ginger Rogers).

Joanne Woodward (1930–)
1117 Tower Road, Beverly Hills

Joanne Woodward worked in TV and on Broadway in the early 1950s, before being cast as a country girl who goes from wild to sedate in *Count Three and Pray* (1955). A few years later Woodward starred in *The Three Faces of Eve* (1957), for which she won the Best Actress Oscar. She also appeared with her husband, Paul Newman, in several films, including *Long Hot Summer* (1958), and was directed by Newman in *Rachel, Rachel* (1968) and other films.

Connecticut has been the permanent home of Woodward and Newman for decades, but they live in Beverly Hills when career demands called for a Hollywood home base. In the early 1960s they lived here, and a few years later they took up residence on Beverly Drive, south of Sunset.

Fay Wray (1907–)
1424 North Beverly Drive, Los Angeles

Fay Wray's most enduring role was that of the screaming blonde who finds herself in the clutches of the monster in *King Kong* (1933). Among Wray's other notable movies were *The Most Dangerous Game* (1932) and *Countess of Monte Cristo* (1934). In later years she had small parts in such movies as *Tammy and the Bachelor* (1957).

Wray lived in this cozy house on the farther reaches of Beverly Drive in the 1950s. When making *King Kong*, her home was an English-style farmhouse (since torn down) on Selma Avenue.

Teresa Wright (1918–)
245 South Crescent Drive, Beverly Hills

In her film debut, Theresa Wright played the daughter of the scheming Bette Davis in *The Little Foxes* (1941). Wright went on to appear in *Mrs. Miniver* (1943) (for which she won the Oscar for Best Supporting Actress), *The Pride of the Yankees* (1942), *Shadow of a Doubt* (1943) and *The Best Years of Our Lives* (1946). In 1988 Wright played Diane Keaton's mother in *The Good Mother*.

Wright lived in this home south of Wilshire during the 1950s. In 1942 her living quarters were simpler. In his 1942 profile of Wright in *Collier's Weekly* magazine, Kyle Crichton wrote, "She lives on the wrong side of the tracks in Beverly Hills and can be reached only by explorers of great fortitude. It will be found that Miss Wright lives somewhere down a driveway. Furthermore, she lives over a garage."

Jane Wyman (1914–)
1323 Miller Drive, Hollywood Hills

Jane Wyman played Ray Milland's girlfriend in the Academy Award-winning film *Lost Weekend* (1945), and three years later won her own Oscar for her

performance as the embattled title character in *Johnny Belinda* (1948). In 1938, Wyman co-starred in *Brother Rat* with Ronald Reagan. They were married two years later.

After Wyman and Reagan were married in 1940, they rented a two-bedroom apartment on the bottom floor of an Art-Moderne building behind this gate. It's located on a private street off of Londonderry View, above Sunset. About three years later the couple built a house two miles west of their Miller Drive apartment. Following their divorce in 1948, Reagan moved back into the apartment.

Gig Young (1913–1978)
919 North Rexford Drive, Beverly Hills

Gig Young had featured roles in such hits as *The Three Musketeers* (1948), *Desk Set* (1957) and *That Touch of Mink* (1962). His performance as the emcee of the dance marathon in *They Shoot Horses, Don't They?* (1969) earned Young the Academy Award for Best Supporting Actor. Audiences, who had come to know Young for his often light-hearted screen personality, were shocked when he killed his wife, and then himself, in 1978.

In the mid-1960s, Young attended a party at 919 North Rexford Drive. During the party he reportedly said to a friend, "I'm just crazy about this house." The house's owner overheard Young and told him it was for sale. Not long afterward, Young bought the house.

Gig Young
919 North Rexford Drive, Beverly Hills

Loretta Young (1913–2000)
El Royale Apartments, 450 North Rossmore Avenue, Hancock Park

Loretta Young built a highly successful career as a refined romantic leading lady. Her first major role was opposite Lon Chaney in the maudlin drama *Laugh Clown Laugh* (1928). She was paired with Douglas Fairbanks, Jr., in several movies, starting with *The Careless Age* (1929). In one of her rare forays into bad-girl parts, Young played an unwed mother in *Born to Be Bad* (1934) with Cary Grant. She appeared with Grant again in the popular *The Bishop's Wife* (1947).

In the early 1930s, Young and her husband, actor Grant Withers, lived at the El Royale Apartments. The 12-story building features elements of Spanish and French Renaissance details. After the couple divorced, Young moved into a Bel Air mansion which her mother, interior designer Gladys Belzer, designed with architect Garrett Van Pelt.

Robert Young (1907–1998)
607 North Elm Drive, Beverly Hills

Robert Young specialized in playing agreeable leading men in such movies as *House of Rothchild* (1933), *Three Comrades* (1938) and *Sitting Pretty* (1948). It turned out that Young's gentle manner lent itself perfectly to the lead in the radio-show-turned-TV-series *Father Knows Best* (1954–1960), followed by TV's *Marcus Welby, M.D.* (1969–1976).

Young lived here during his *Father Knows Best* years. In 1974 he and his wife, Betty, built a house in Westlake Village and relocated there.

Robert Young
607 North Elm Drive, Beverly Hills

Map of the Los Angeles Area

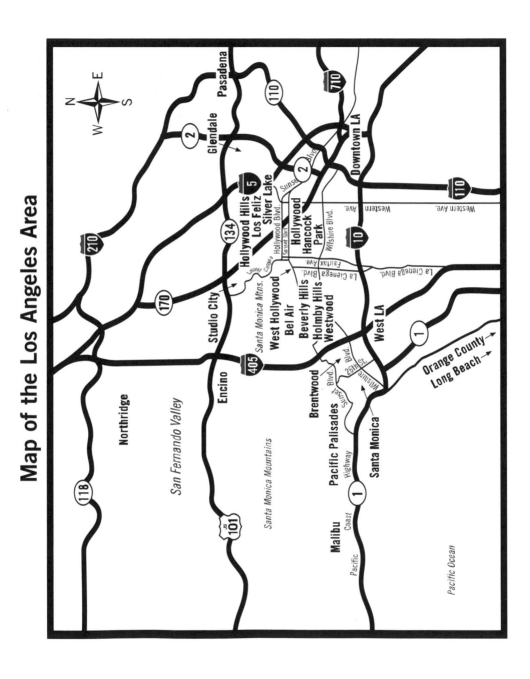

APPENDIX

Movie Star Homes by Region

Beverly Hills and Vicinity

Dana Andrews
Ann-Margret
Fred Astaire
Lauren Bacall
Lucille Ball
Theda Bara
Lex Barker
Lionel Barrymore
Warner Baxter
Warren Beatty
Ralph Bellamy
Joan Bennett
Jack Benny
Candice Bergen
Edgar Bergen
Ingrid Bergman
Joan Blondell
Monte Blue
Humphrey Bogart
Ray Bolger
Shirley Booth
Olive Borden
Clara Bow
Charles Bronson
Joe E. Brown
John Mack Brown
Nigel Bruce
James Cagney
Michael Caine
Rory Calhoun
Jeff Chandler
Lon Chaney
Lon Chaney, Jr.
Charlie Chaplin
Ruth Chatterton
Ruth Clifford
Rosemary Clooney
Lee J. Cobb
Lew Cody
James Coburn
Claudette Colbert
Betty Compson
Richard Conte
Gary Cooper
Jackie Cooper
Bob Cummings
Tony Curtis
Karl Dane

Marion Davies
Sammy Davis, Jr.
Doris Day
Laraine Day
Marlene Dietrich
Richard Dix
Kirk Douglas
Marie Dressler
Faye Dunaway
Jimmy Durante
Clint Eastwood
Peter Falk
Mia Farrow
W.C. Fields
Carrie Fisher
Henry Fonda
Glenn Ford
Harrison Ford
Greta Garbo
Greer Garson
Mitzi Gaynor
Paulette Goddard
Cary Grant
Corrine Griffith
Buddy Hackett
Jack Haley
George Hamilton
Oliver Hardy
Richard Harris
Audrey Hepburn
Katharine Hepburn
Leslie Howard
Van Johnson
Shirley Jones
Boris Karloff
Danny Kaye
Gene Kelly

Alan Ladd
Diane Ladd
Bert Lahr
Veronica Lake
Hedy Lamarr
Dorothy Lamour
Stan Laurel
Janet Leigh
Jack Lemmon
Oscar Levant
Jeanette MacDonald
Dorothy Malone
Herbert Marshall
Raymond Massey
Chico Marx
Groucho Marx
Harpo Marx
Zeppo Marx
James Mason
Victor Mature
Darrin McGavin
Dorothy McGuire
Adolph Menjou
Bette Midler
Ray Milland
Ann Miller
Yvette Mimieux
Marilyn Monroe
George Montgomery
Robert Montgomery
Agnes Moorehead
Frank Morgan
Alan Mowbray
Eddie Murphy
George Murphy
Carmel Myers
Paul Newman

Anna Q. Nilsson
Mabel Normand
Merle Oberon
Maureen O'Hara
Maureen O'Sullivan
Jack Palance
Eleanor Parker
Walter Pidgeon
Brad Pitt
Sidney Poitier
Dick Powell
William Powell
Elvis Presley
Vincent Price
Martha Raye
Donna Reed
George Reeves
Burt Reynolds
Edward G. Robinson
Ginger Rogers
Gilbert Roland
Rosalind Russell
Ann Rutherford
Eva Marie Saint
Joseph Schildkraut
George C. Scott
Phil Silvers
Frank Sinatra
Elke Sommer
James Spader
Robert Stack
James Stewart
Barbra Streisand
Blanche Sweet
Akim Tamiroff
Elizabeth Taylor
Rod Taylor

Lana Turner
Ben Turpin
Rudolph Valentino
Conrad Veidt
Shelley Winters
James Woods
Joanne Woodward
Fay Wray
Teresa Wright
Gig Young
Robert Young

Brentwood
June Allyson
Billie Burke
Jim Carrey
Charley Chase
Joan Crawford
Nelson Eddy
James Garner
Van Heflin
Paul Henreid
Ida Lupino
Fred MacMurray
Robert Morse
Gregory Peck
Mary Pickford
ZaSu Pitts
Tyrone Power
Robert Preston
Charles "Buddy" Rogers
Donald Sutherland
Shirley Temple
Richard Widmark
Esther Williams

Glendale
John Wayne

**Hollywood/Hollywood Hills/
West Hollywood**
Eve Arden
Mary Astor
Lucille Ball
Anne Bancroft
Kathy Bates
Anne Baxter
William Boyd
Marlon Brando
Louise Brooks
Mel Brooks
Steve Buscemi
Mae Busch
James Cagney
Marge and Gower Champion
Charlie Chaplin
Virginia Cherrill
Charles Coburn
Gary Cooper
Broderick Crawford
Dorothy Dandridge
Bette Davis
Richard Dreyfuss
Deanna Durbin
Dan Duryea
Errol Flynn
Ava Gardner
Judy Garland
Janet Gaynor
Leo Gorcey
Sidney Greenstreet
William "Billy" Haines
Alan Hale

Margaret Hamilton
William S. Hart
William Holden
Kim Hunter
Tab Hunter
Grace Kelly
J. Warren Kerrigan
Percy Kilbride
Barbara La Marr
Elsa Lancaster
Charles Laughton
Beatrice Lillie
Peter Lorre
Bela Lugosi
Steve McQueen
Sal Mineo
Marilyn Monroe
Kim Novak
Ramon Novarro
Anthony Perkins
Joe Roberts
Ruth Roland
Roy Schieder
Randolph Scott
Harry Dean Stanton
Jan Sterling
Sharon Stone
Grady Sutton
Norma Talmadge
Spencer Tracy
Helen Twelvetrees
Lupe Velez
John Wayne
Orson Welles
Natalie Wood
Jane Wyman

Long Beach
Robert Mitchum

**Los Angeles: Central/
Downtown/Hancock Park**
Eddie "Rochester" Anderson
Fatty Arbuckle
Drew Barrymore
John Barrymore
Richard Barthelmess
Miriam Cooper
Ann Dvorak
John Gilbert
Lillian Gish
Buster Keaton
Harold Lloyd
Hattie McDaniel
Colleen Moore
Jack Pickford
Mary Pickford
Edna Purviance
George Raft
Rudolph Valentino
Mae West
Loretta Young

Los Feliz
Danny DeVito
Clark Gable
Betty Grable
Oliver Hardy
Basil Rathbone
Gloria Swanson

Malibu
Lou Gossett, Jr.
Nick Nolte

Mulholland Drive Area
Julie Andrews
Warren Beatty
Annette Bening
Joan Fontaine
Rex Harrison
Charleton Heston
Myrna Loy
Jack Nicholson

Orange County
Buddy Ebsen

Pacific Palisades/Santa Monica
Eric Blore
Jeff Bridges
Joseph Cotten
Tom Cruise
Billy Crystal
Bebe Daniels
Marion Davies
Dolores Del Rio
Billie Dove
Douglas Fairbanks
Douglas Fairbanks, Jr.
Tom Hanks
Goldie Hawn
Nicole Kidman
Peter Lawford
Harold Lloyd
Walter Matthau
Mary Miles Minter
David Niven
Anthony Quinn
Ronald Reagan
Arnold Schwarzenegger
Norma Shearer

Sylvester Stallone
Norma Talmadge
Robert Taylor
Shirley Temple
Thelma Todd
Johnny Weissmuller

San Fernando Valley
Bud Abbott
Don Ameche
Gene Autry
Kim Basinger
Ernest Borgnine
Dana Carvey
George Clooney
Lou Costello
Bing Crosby
William Demarest
Annette Funicello
Clark Gable
Cuba Gooding, Jr.
Virginia Grey
Susan Hayward
Bob Hope
Bo Hopkins
Samuel L. Jackson
Al Jolson
Francis Lederer
Carole Lombard
Shirley MacLaine
Roddy McDowall
Robert Mitchum
Jack Oakie
Mickey Rooney
Lee Van Cleef
Robert Wagner
Denzel Washington

Silver Lake
Judy Garland
Tom Mix

West Los Angeles
Joan Crawford
Brian Donlevy
Sally Eilers
Jean Harlow
Patricia Neal

Westwood
James Dean
Ben Gazzara
Debbie Reynolds
Barbara Stanwyck

Movie Star Homes: Theme Tours

The Femme Fatale Tour
Beverly Hills and Vicinity
Ann-Margret
Theda Bara
Olive Borden
Clara Bow
Hedy Lamarr
Yvette Mimieux
Marilyn Monroe (see also
   Hollywood/Hollywood
   Hills/West Hollywood)
Elke Sommer
Elizabeth Taylor
Lana Turner

**Hollywood/Hollywood Hills/
West Hollywood**
Louise Brooks
Ava Gardner
Marilyn Monroe (see also
  Beverly Hills and Vicinity)
Kim Novak
Sharon Stone
Natalie Wood

Los Feliz
Betty Grable

Pacific Palisades/Santa Monica
Dolores Del Rio
Thelma Todd

San Fernando Valley
Kim Basinger
Carole Lombard

West Los Angeles
Jean Harlow

The Hunk Tour
Beverly Hills and Vicinity
Cary Grant
Charlton Heston
Paul Newman
Brad Pitt
Rudolph Valentino (see also
  Los Angeles)

Brentwood
Gregory Peck
Tyrone Power

**Los Angeles: Central/
Downtown/Hancock Park**
Richard Barthelmess
John Gilbert
Rudolph Valentino (see also
  Beverly Hills and Vicinity)

**Hollywood/Hollywood Hills/
West Hollywood**
Errol Flynn
Tab Hunter
Ramon Novarro

Los Feliz
Clark Gable (see also San
  Fernando Valley)

Pacific Palisades/Santa Monica
Tom Cruise
Arnold Schwarzenegger
Robert Taylor

San Fernando Valley
George Clooney
Clark Gable (see also Los Feliz)
Denzel Washington

The Silent Tour
Beverly Hills and Vicinity
Theda Bara
Monte Blue
Olive Borden
Clara Bow
Lon Chaney
Charlie Chaplin (see also
  Hollywood/Hollywood
  Hills/West Hollywood)

Lew Cody
Betty Compson
Karl Dane
Marion Davies (see also Beverly Hills and Vicinity)
Richard Dix
Corrine Griffith
Carmel Myers
Anna Q. Nilsson
Mabel Normand
Blanche Sweet
Ben Turpin
Rudolph Valentino (see also Los Angeles)

Brentwood
Charley Chase
Mary Pickford (see also Los Angeles)

Hollywood/Hollywood Hills/ West Hollywood
Louise Brooks
Mae Busch
Charlie Chaplin (see also Beverly Hills and Vicinity)
Virginia Cherrill
William "Billy" Haines
William S. Hart
J. Warren Kerrigan
Barbara La Marr
Ramon Novarro
Joe Roberts
Ruth Roland
Norma Talmadge (see also Pacific Palisades and Santa Monica)

Los Angeles: Central/ Downtown/Hancock Park
Fatty Arbuckle
John Barrymore
Richard Barthelmess
Miriam Cooper
John Gilbert
Lillian Gish
Buster Keaton
Harold Lloyd (see also Pacific Palisades and Santa Monica)
Colleen Moore
Mary Pickford (see also Brentwood)
Jack Pickford
Edna Purviance
Rudolph Valentino (see also Beverly Hills and Vicinity)

Pacific Palisades/Santa Monica
Billie Dove
Babe Daniels
Marion Davies (see also Beverly Hills and Vicinity)
Douglas Fairbanks
Harold Lloyd (see also Los Angeles)
Mary Miles Minter
Norma Talmadge (see also Hollywood/Hollywood Hills/West Hollywood)
Thelma Todd

Silver Lake
Tom Mix

The Musical Tour
Beverly Hills and Vicinity
Julie Andrews
Ann-Margret
Fred Astaire
Ray Bolger
Rosemary Clooney
Sammy Davis, Jr.
Doris Day
Marlene Dietrich
Mitzi Gaynor
Shirley Jones
Gene Kelly
Oscar Levant
Jeanette MacDonald
Bette Midler
Ann Miller
George Murphy
Dick Powell
Elvis Presley
Martha Raye
Ginger Rogers
Frank Sinatra
Barbra Streisand

Brentwood
Nelson Eddy
Robert Preston
Shirley Temple (see also Pacific
  Palisades and Santa Monica)

Los Feliz
Betty Grable

**Hollywood/Hollywood Hills/
West Hollywood**
Marge and Gower Champion
Dorothy Dandridge

Deanna Durbin
Judy Garland (see also Silver
  Lake)
Lupe Velez

Pacific Palisades/Santa Monica
Shirley Temple (see also
  Brentwood)

Silver Lake
Judy Garland (see also
  Brentwood)

San Fernando Valley
Bing Crosby
Annette Funicello

Westwood
Debbie Reynolds

Movie Star Homes: Tours by Films
Note: in the following tours, the name of the character played by each actor is in parentheses.

Birth of a Nation (1915)
Beverly Hills and Vicinity
Monte Blue (extra)

**Los Angeles: Central/
Downtown/Hancock Park**
Miriam Cooper (Margaret
  Cameron)
Lillian Gish (Elsie Stoneman)

Casablanca (1942)
Beverly Hills and Vicinity
Ingrid Bergman (Ilsa Lund Laszlo)
Monte Blue (unnamed American)
Humphrey Bogart (Rick Blaine)
Conrad Veidt (Maj. Heinrich
　Strasser)

Brentwood
Paul Henreid (Victor Laszlo)

**Hollywood/Hollywood Hills/
West Hollywood**
Sidney Greenstreet (Signor
　Ferrari)
Peter Lorre (Guillermo Ugarte)

Citizen Kane (1941)
Beverly Hills and Vicinity
Agnes Moorehead (Mrs. Mary
　Kane)
Alan Ladd (unnamed reporter)

**Hollywood/Hollywood Hills/
West Hollywood**
Orson Welles (Charles Foster
　Kane)

Pacific Palisades/Santa Monica
Joseph Cotten (Jedediah
　Leland)

Dial M for Murder (1954)
Beverly Hills and Vicinity
Robert Cummings (Mark
　Halliday)
Ray Milland (Tony Wendice)

**Hollywood/Hollywood Hills/
West Hollywood**
Grace Kelly (Margot Mary
　Wendice)

Gone With the Wind (1939)
Beverly Hills and Vicinity
Leslie Howard (Ashley Wilkes)
George Reeves (Stuart Tarleton)
Ann Rutherford (Carreen
　O'Hara)

**Los Angeles: Central/
Downtown/Hancock Park**
Eddie "Rochester" Anderson
　(Uncle Peter)
Hattie McDaniel (Mammy)

Los Feliz
Clark Gable (Rhett Butler) (see
　also San Fernando Valley)

San Fernando Valley
Clark Gable (Rhett Butler) (see
　also Los Feliz)

The Great Escape (1963)
Beverly Hills and Vicinity
Charles Bronson (Lt. Danny
  "The Tunnel King" Velinski)
James Coburn (Ofcr. Louis
  "The Manufacturer" Sedgwick)

Brentwood
James Garner (Lt. Bob Anthony
  "The Scrounger" Hendley)

**Hollywood/Hollywood Hills/
West Hollywood**
Steve McQueen (Capt. Virgil
  "The Cooler King" Hilts)

❖

It's a Mad Mad Mad Mad World (1963)
Beverly Hills and Vicinity
Jack Benny (unnamed man in car
  in the desert)
Joe E. Brown (unnamed union
  official)
Jimmy Durante (Smiler Grogan)
Peter Falk (unnamed third cab
  driver)
Buddy Hackett (Benjy Benjamin)
Phil Silvers (Otto Meyer)

Brentwood
ZaSu Pitts (Gertie)

**Hollywood/Hollywood Hills/
West Hollywood**
Leo Gorcey (unnamed first cab
  driver)

Spencer Tracy (Capt. T.G.
  Culpeper)

**Los Angeles: Central/
Downtown/Hancock Park**
Eddie "Rochester" Anderson
  (unnamed second cab driver)
Buster Keaton (Jimmy the
  boatman)

San Fernando Valley
William Demarest (Police chief
  Aloysius)
Mickey Rooney (Ding "Dingy"
  Bell)

❖

It's a Wonderful Life (1946)
Beverly Hills and Vicinity
James Stewart (George Bailey)
Donna Reed (Mary Hatch Bailey)
Lionel Barrymore (Mr. Potter)

❖

MacKenna's Gold (1969)
Beverly Hills and Vicinity
Lee J. Cobb (unnamed editor)
Raymond Massey (unnamed
  preacher)
Edward G. Robinson (Old
  Adams)

Brentwood
Gregory Peck (MacKenna)

❖

Ocean's Eleven (1960 and 2001)
Beverly Hills and Vicinity
Richard Conte (Anthony "Tony" Bergdorf)
Sammy Davis, Jr. (Josh Howard)
Brad Pitt (Rusty Ryan)
Frank Sinatra (Danny Ocean)
Akim Tamiroff (Spyros Acebos)

Los Angeles: Central/ Downtown/Hancock Park
George Raft (Jack Strager)

Pacific Palisades/Santa Monica
Peter Lawford (Jimmy Foster)

San Fernando Valley
George Clooney (Danny Ocean
Shirley MacLaine (Tipsy girl)

❖

On the Waterfront (1954)
Beverly Hills and Vicinity
Lee J. Cobb (Johnny Friendly)
Eva Marie Saint (Edie Doyle)

Mulholland Drive Area
Marlon Brando (Terry Malloy)

❖

Shane (1953)
Beverly Hills and Vicinity
Jack Palance (Jack Wilson)
Alan Ladd (Shane)

Brentwood
Van Heflin (Joe Starrett)

❖

Show People (1928)
Beverly Hills and Vicinity
Charlie Chaplin (cameo appearance) (see also Hollywood/ Hollywood Hills/West Hollywood)
Lew Cody (cameo appearance)
Karl Dane (cameo appearance)
Marion Davies (Peggy Pepper) (see also Pacific Palisades and Santa Monica)

Hollywood/Hollywood Hills/ West Hollywood
Charlie Chaplin (cameo appearance) (see also Beverly Hills and Vicinity)
William "Billy" Haines (Billy Boone)
William S. Hart (cameo appearance)
Norma Talmadge (cameo appearance) (see also Pacific Palisades and Santa Monica)

Los Angeles: Central/ Downtown/Hancock Park
John Gilbert (cameo appearance)

Pacific Palisades/Santa Monica
Marion Davies (Peggy Pepper) (see also Beverly Hills and Vicinity)

❖

Douglas Fairbanks (cameo appearance)
Norma Talmadge (cameo appearance) (see also Hollywood/Hollywood Hills/West Hollywood)

❖

Some Like It Hot (1959)
Beverly Hills and Vicinity
Joe E. Brown (Osgood Fielding)
Tony Curtis (Joe/Josephine)
Jack Lemmon (Jerry/Daphne)
Marilyn Monroe (Sugar Kane Kowalczyk) (see also Hollywood/Hollywood Hills/West Hollywood)
Edward G. Robinson (Johnny Paradise)

Hollywood/Hollywood Hills/ West Hollywood
Marilyn Monroe (Sugar Kane Kowalczyk) (see also Beverly Hills and Vicinity)

Los Angeles: Central/ Downtown/Hancock Park
George Raft (Spats Colombo)

❖

Sunset Boulevard (1950)
Beverly Hills and Vicinity
Ruth Clifford (unnamed secretary)
Anna Q. Nilsson (herself)

Hollywood/Hollywood Hills/ West Hollywood
William Holden (Joe Gillis)

Los Angeles: Central/ Downtown/Hancock Park
Buster Keaton (himself)

Los Feliz
Gloria Swanson (Norma Desmond)

❖

Wings (1927)
Beverly Hills and Vicinity
Clara Bow (Mary Preston)
Gary Cooper (Cadet White) (see also Hollywood/Hollywood Hills/West Hollywood)

Hollywood/Hollywood Hills/ West Hollywood
Gary Cooper (Cadet White) (see also Beverly Hills and Vicinity)

Brentwood
Charles "Buddy" Rogers (Jack Powell)

❖

The Wizard of Oz (1939)
Beverly Hills and Vicinity
Ray Bolger (The Scarecrow/Hunk)
Jack Haley (The Tin Man/ Hickory)

Bert Lahr (The Cowardly
Lion/Zeke)
Frank Morgan (The Wizard of
Oz/The Wizard's guard/Cab
driver/Emerald City doorman/
Prof. Marvel)

Brentwood
Billie Burke (Glinda, the Good
Witch of the North)

Silver Lake
Judy Garland (Dorothy Gale)
(see also Hollywood/
Hollywood Hills/West
Hollywood)

**Hollywood/Hollywood Hills/
West Hollywood**
Judy Garland (Dorothy Gale)
(see also Silver Lake)
Margaret Hamilton (The
Wicked Witch of the
West/Almira Gulch)

Brentwood
Joan Crawford (Crystal Allen)
(see also West Los Angeles and
Vicinity)

Mulholland Drive Area
Joan Fontaine (Mrs. John
Day—Peggy)

San Fernando Valley
Virginia Grey (Pat, the perfume
counter clerk)

Pacific Palisades/Santa Monica
Norma Shearer (Mrs. Stephen
Haines—Mary)

West Los Angeles and Vicinity
Joan Crawford (Crystal Allen)
(see also Brentwood)

The Women (1939)
Beverly Hills and Vicinity
(includes Bel Air and Holmby
Hills)
Paulette Goddard (Miriam
Aarons)
Rosalind Russell (Mrs. Howard
Fowler—Sylvia)

BIBLIOGRAPHY

Architectural Digest, Academy Award Collectors Edition. April 1990, April 1992.

_____, Hollywood At Home. April 1994, April 1996, April 1998, April 2000.

Gebhard, David and Winter, Robert. *A Guide to Architecture in Los Angeles and Southern California.* Salt Lake City: Peregrine Smith, 1977.

Herr, Jeffrey, and City of Los Angeles. *Landmark L.A.* Santa Monica: Angel City Press, 2002.

Internet Movie Database, http://www.imdb.com/

Kashner, Sam and MacNair, Jennifer. *The Bad & The Beautiful.* W.W. Norton & Company, 2003.

Knight, Arthur and Elisofon, Eliot. *The Hollywood Style.* London: The MacMillan Company, 1969.

Lamparski, Richard. *Lamparksi's Hidden Hollywood.* New York: Simon & Schuster, 1981.

Lockwood, Charles. *Dream Palaces: Hollywood at Home.* New York: Viking, 1981.

_____. *The Guide to Hollywood and Beverly Hills.* New York: Crown Publishers, Inc. 1984.

Monush, Barry. *The Encyclopedia of Hollywood Film Actors from the Silent Era to 1965*. Applause Theatre & Cinema Books, 2003.

Ovnick, Merry. *Los Angeles: The End of the Rainbow*. Los Angeles: Balcony Press, 1994.

Slide, Anthony. *Silent Players*. Lexington, Ky.: The University Press of Kentucky, 2002.

Torrence, Bruce. *Hollywood: The First 100 Years*. Hollywood, Calif.: Hollywood Chamber of Commerce and Fiske Enterprises, 1979.

Wallace, David. *Hollywoodland*. New York: L.A. Weekly Books/St. Martin's Press, 2002.

_____. *Lost Hollywood*. New York: L.A. Weekly Books/St. Martin's Press, 2001.

ACKNOWLEDGMENTS

This seemingly simple book was, in fact, a complicated undertaking. Our work involved solving mysteries and tracking down facts that would have taken us years without the resources of such organizations as The Los Angeles Public Library, The Academy of Motion Picture Arts and Sciences' Margaret Herrick Library and The Santa Monica Historical Society Museum. We are also indebted to the following people who cheerfully shared with us their time, insights, expertise and moral support:

Alyssa Artunian, John Bengston, Linda Brady and June Lewin of The Beverly Hills Public Library, Ron Cherney, Philip Collins, Bryan Cooper, Judy Cooper, Beverly Cressey, Barbara Hall of The Margaret Herrick Library, Jan Eric Horn of Coldwell Banker's Architectural Division, Amelia Ostroff, Victoria Sainte-Claire of The Damfinos: The International Buster Keaton Society, Glenn Taranto of richarddix.com, Kay Tornborg of Hollywood Heritage, Leo Walters of mary-miles-minter.com, Marc Wanamaker of Bison Archives.

We are also grateful to our families for their ongoing enthusiasm and encouragement. A special thank you to Gene, Sherrie and Kara Oldham; Katie Robino; and Gladys, Rich, Stephanie, Adam and April Artunian.

Judy Artunian (1952–)
1788 North Summit Avenue, Pasadena

After a year-long stint as a newsroom assistant at KFWB radio in Los Angeles, Judy Artunian spent 14 years in public relations. She switched careers again in 1992 when she became a freelance writer. Artunian has since written hundreds of articles, including: "Do Short Women Have a Secret Advantage?" (*Glamour*, 1994), "Honey, I Shrunk the Web" (*Tech Trends*, 2000), and "When Does Frugal Become Cheap?" (*Chicago Tribune*, 2003). Artunian's fascination with Hollywood history was sparked during her teen years when she read Colleen Moore's memoir, *Silent Star*.

Artunian lived here for the first year of her life. In those days, the clapboard house, which belonged to her grandparents, Mike and Sarah, was painted white. The porch stretched across the front of the house. According to Artunian's mother, Gladys, "We used to put Judy in the playpen in the breakfast nook, which was very spacious. One of her favorite pastimes in the playpen was crumpling up newspaper pages. Her grandmother was the one who discovered that the newspaper would stop Judy from crying. That was the beginning of Judy's literary career."

Mike Oldham (1958–)
177 South Jameson Street, Orange

Mike Oldham was in grammar school when he made his first foray into Beverly Hills to tour film star homes with his family. Oldham has pursued a career that is a world away from Hollywood. After earning an MBA in the mid-1980s, he went into sales, eventually becoming the managing partner of a wholesale distributorship.

In the summer of 1958, Oldham was a newborn when his parents brought him home to this duplex. It was painted a sunny yellow, just as it is today. Oldham's mother, Sherrie, described the unit as, "Ultra-modern, with knotty-pine cabinets and hardwood floors. It was the cat's meow. The rent was $90 a month and that was expensive then. The back door led right out into a cute backyard that had clothes lines, and Mike used to sit out there squinting in the sun in the playpen."

You may contact the authors at hollywoodlandings@sbcglobal.net.

Books Available
from Santa Monica Press

Blues for Bird
by Martin Gray
288 pages $16.95

The Book of Good Habits
*Simple and Creative Ways to Enrich
Your Life*
by Dirk Mathison
224 pages $9.95

The Butt Hello
*and other ways my cats
drive me crazy*
by Ted Meyer
96 pages $9.95

Café Nation
*Coffee Folklore, Magick,
and Divination*
by Sandra Mizumoto Posey
224 pages $9.95

Cats Around the World
by Ted Meyer
96 pages $9.95

Childish Things
by Davis & Davis
96 pages $19.95

**Discovering the History of Your
House**
and Your Neighborhood
by Betsy J. Green
288 pages $14.95

The Dog Ate My Resumé
by Zack Arnstein and Larry
Arnstein
192 pages $11.95

Dogme Uncut
*Lars von Trier, Thomas Vinterberg
and the Gang That Took on
Hollywood*
by Jack Stevenson
312 pages $16.95

**Exotic Travel Destinations for
Families**
by Jennifer M. Nichols and Bill
Nichols
360 pages $16.95

Footsteps in the Fog
Alfred Hitchcock's San Francisco
by Jeff Kraft and
Aaron Leventhal
240 pages $24.95

**Free Stuff & Good Deals for
Folks over 50, 2nd Ed.**
by Linda Bowman
240 pages $12.95

**How to Find Your Family Roots
and Write Your Family History**
by William Latham and
Cindy Higgins
288 pages $14.95

How to Speak Shakespeare
by Cal Pritner and
Louis Colaianni
144 pages $16.95

**How to Win Lotteries, Sweepstakes,
and Contests in the 21st Century**
by Steve "America's Sweepstakes
King" Ledoux
224 pages $14.95

**Jackson Pollock:
Memories Arrested in Space**
by Martin Gray
216 pages $14.95

James Dean Died Here
*The Locations of America's Pop
Culture Landmarks*
by Chris Epting
312 pages $16.95

The Keystone Kid
Tales of Early Hollywood
by Coy Watson, Jr.
312 pages $24.95

Letter Writing Made Easy!
*Featuring Sample Letters for
Hundreds of Common Occasions*
by Margaret McCarthy
224 pages $12.95

**Letter Writing Made Easy!
Volume 2**
*Featuring More Sample Letters for
Hundreds of Common Occasions*
by Margaret McCarthy
224 pages $12.95

Life is Short. Eat Biscuits!
by Amy Jordan Smith
96 pages $9.95

Marilyn Monroe Dyed Here
*More Locations of America's
Pop Culture Landmarks*
by Chris Epting
312 pages $16.95

Movie Star Homes
by Judy Artunian and Mike
Oldham
312 pages $16.95

Offbeat Food
*Adventures in an
Omnivorous World*
by Alan Ridenour
240 pages $19.95

Offbeat Marijuana
*The Life and Times of the
World's Grooviest Plant*
by Saul Rubin
240 pages $19.95

Offbeat Museums
*The Collections and Curators of
America's Most Unusual Museums*
by Saul Rubin
240 pages $19.95

A Prayer for Burma
by Kenneth Wong
216 pages $14.95

Quack!
*Tales of Medical Fraud from the
Museum of Questionable Medical
Devices*
by Bob McCoy
240 pages $19.95

Redneck Haiku
by Mary K. Witte
112 pages $9.95

**School Sense: How to Help Your
Child Succeed in Elementary
School**
by Tiffani Chin, Ph.D.
408 pages $16.95

Silent Echoes
*Discovering Early Hollywood
Through the Films of Buster Keaton*
by John Bengtson
240 pages $24.95

Tiki Road Trip
*A Guide to Tiki Culture in
North America*
by James Teitelbaum
288 pages $16.95

Order Form 1-800-784-9553

	Quantity	Amount
Blues for Bird (epic poem about Charlie Parker) ($16.95)		
The Book of Good Habits ($9.95)		
The Butt Hello . . . and Other Ways My Cats Drive Me Crazy ($9.95)		
Café Nation: Coffee Folklore, Magick and Divination ($9.95)		
Cats Around the World ($9.95)		
Childish Things ($19.95)		
Discovering the History of Your House. . . ($14.95)		
The Dog Ate My Resumé ($11.95)		
Dogme Uncut ($16.95)		
Exotic Travel Destinations for Families ($16.95)		
Footsteps in the Fog: Alfred Hitchcock's San Francisco ($24.95)		
Free Stuff & Good Deals for Folks over 50, 2nd Ed. ($12.95)		
How to Find Your Family Roots . . . ($14.95)		
How to Speak Shakespeare ($16.95)		
How to Win Lotteries, Sweepstakes, and Contests . . . ($14.95)		
Jackson Pollock: Memories Arrested in Space ($14.95)		
James Dean Died Here: America's Pop Culture Landmarks ($16.95)		
The Keystone Kid: Tales of Early Hollywood ($24.95)		
Letter Writing Made Easy! ($12.95)		
Letter Writing Made Easy! Volume 2 ($12.95)		
Life is Short. Eat Biscuits! ($9.95)		
Marilyn Monroe Dyed Here ($16.95)		
Movie Star Homes ($16.95)		
Offbeat Food ($19.95)		
Offbeat Marijuana ($19.95)		
Offbeat Museums ($19.95)		
A Prayer for Burma ($14.95)		
Quack! Tales of Medical Fraud ($19.95)		
Redneck Haiku ($9.95)		
School Sense ($16.95)		
Silent Echoes: Early Hollywood Through Buster Keaton ($24.95)		
Tiki Road Trip ($16.95)		

Subtotal	
CA residents add 8.25% sales tax	
Shipping and Handling (see left)	
TOTAL	

Shipping & Handling:
1 book $3.00
Each additional book is $ .50

Name ——————————————————————————

Address ——————————————————————————

City ————————————— State ————— Zip ——————

❏ Visa ❏ MasterCard Card No.: ——————————————————

Exp. Date ————————— Signature ——————————————

❏ Enclosed is my check or money order payable to:

Santa Monica Press LLC
P.O. Box 1076
Santa Monica, CA 90406
www.santamonicapress.com 1-800-784-9553